Encountering
THE EDGE

WHAT PEOPLE TOLD ME
BEFORE THEY DIED

HOSPICE CHAPLAIN
KAREN B. KAPLAN

P

Pen-L Publishing
Fayetteville, AR
Pen-L.com

First Edition Printed and bound in USA
ISBN: 978-1-940222-35-6

Cover design and Photography by Kelsey Rice
Interior by Kelsey Rice

Dedication

To my brother Steven Bookman, who has nurtured my sensitivity to the written word, and who has fostered my growth as a writer and as a caring person since my teenage years.

Encountering
THE EDGE

WHAT PEOPLE TOLD ME
BEFORE THEY DIED

Table of Contents

Introduction

"HEY DOLL!"
Barney's Unconventional Greeting

As I walked into Barney's room a few doors down from the nursing home lobby, the last thing he wanted from me was pious talk. Knowing that I was a rabbi added an extra kick for the way he greeted me. You see, every time I visited him, he tested me with a forbidden-fruit glance and called out, "Hey doll!" Given the circumstances of Barney being in Act 3 Scene 3 of his life, I was charmed rather than offended. When we had first become acquainted, he was so surprised a woman could be a rabbi.

"I guess I wasn't in the know about these kinds of things," he said, looking embarrassed. "It's been a long time since I've had anything to do with Jewish stuff."

When I asked him why that was, he hinted at a life permeated with shady dealings. Skirting the edge of legal and illegal activities, he had drifted from place to place. Now homeless, he had no place left to go but this nursing home in a Newark neighborhood so iffy, the only safe time for me to drop by was in the morning.

The hospice social worker educated me that criminal types like to sleep in and get their day started in the afternoon. As it was, I saw a dense line of police cars just blocks away from the nursing home, primed for another tumultuous day.

Some weeks later, during one of my last visits with Barney, I hazarded a reference to some Jewish songs and prayers. He was stunned that a prayer beginning with "Hear O Israel" (the most well-known Jewish prayer and referred to in Hebrew as "the Shema") sounded familiar. Hearing me talk about prayers he had not heard for decades, he was taken aback that they comforted him. "Funny how things come in a circle," he reflected. "I heard Hebrew when I was a little kid, and now," he made a face signifying that he did not have long to live, "I'm hearing about it again." He had come home to his Jewish heritage.

At our last visit several weeks later, Barney was almost unconscious. The nurses on the morning shift said he was not responding anymore. But when I came in and said, "Hey doll!" he lifted his left brow and smiled ever so slightly before resuming his voyage onward in the untroubled waters. I sat with him awhile, thinking about my own penchant for flirting with the playful aspects of religion, and for having sought out a vocation that would be full of surprises at every turn.

Throughout my seven-year career of encountering people at death's door, friends and family have puzzled over my offbeat choice of career. "Isn't it depressing? Doesn't it get you down?" easily take first place for the most frequently asked questions. Other top contenders I get include:

"What do people near the end want to talk about?"

"What do you say to them?"

"What wisdom do they share?"

"Come crunch time, what do they really believe will happen to them?"

"How do they cope with knowing their time is near?"

And one of my own favorites, which even the patients themselves ask:

"Why do you want to do this kind of work?" (Read: "Why on earth would you want to? You must be a little strange.")

Some people persist with even more intrusive inquiries such as, "Doesn't this work make you think about your own mortality a lot? Have you ever seen anyone die right in front of you?" And most aggressive and most revealing of all about the questioner's fear of death: "Are you sure you should be writing a book like this?" Some people have been so upset about my writing this career memoir, you would think I had self-sabotaged hopes of finding an audience for this book by calling it *Disturbing Confessions of a Hospice Chaplain: Terrifying Tales.*

But then again, you may be curious about how my visits with people from all walks of life have shaped my beliefs about the meaning of life and the nature of the hereafter. You might wonder what you would witness if you could invisibly accompany me on my visits. You might wonder what it is like to constantly improvise how to respond depending on the patient's personality, mood, presence of family or of medical professionals, ethnic and racial background, and even socioeconomic level.

If you are nevertheless ambivalent about reading about this subject any further, it may hearten you to know how I myself reacted when United Hospice of Rockland in New City, New York made me my first hospice employment offer in 2005. It does not take much to imagine how I hesitated over this sharp turn in my career from pulpit to bedside. What was I getting myself into? Talk about encounters with the edge! I took a deep enough breath that would have pleased any yoga instructor and told the interviewer, yes (slowly exhale), I'd take the position. She told me the job would start the very next day, so I did not even have any time to emotionally transition from leading a congregation to being a chaplain under a nursing supervisor in the rule-filled world of health care.

But the result of that yes has often been privileged access to persons and their families during some of the more intimate and meaningful moments of their lives. What you will see here are recollections of some of these slices of life: some humorous in their own right, some edgy, some peaceful, some sad, some odd, and some uplifting. You will also find an inside look at spiritual and emotional issues that arise in hospice care, such as interfaith conflict, remorse, doubt, and guilt. These are not so much stories about death as they are about people's lives in the moment I see them. They reminisce over their experiences, thoughts, and actions whether past or present. They care about family issues just as we all do at any other stage of our lives. The aim of each anecdote in this book is to portray how the moments in question were adventurous, inspiring, meaningful, perplexing, or otherwise authentic to those present. As you peruse these tales, you may in turn have these reactions, or at least get a glimpse into a time of life that was a fertile ground for the patient's search for meaning and for the affirmation of what each valued most.

When I told friends and family that I was going to write about my encounters as a chaplain, one friend cheered me on saying I would be preserving intimate spiritual events that many people would otherwise not know about. Moreover, he said this collection of stories would be my legacy. Mentioning my legacy is fittingly ironic, as much of my job is to encourage others to ponder what their legacy is, and to construct their life's meaning by doing so. For me to be the one considering my own is a deserved challenge.

Unlike many other books I have seen about hospice chaplaincy, this one is not about inserting any agenda overt or hidden to influence your religious beliefs or non-beliefs one way or the other. Some people are unaware that professionally trained chaplains do not visit clients to preach or persuade them of the superiority of a specific religion. As you will see, I aim to be like an amplifier that boosts and affirms the spiritual and emotional self-awareness of those I serve, whatever their beliefs, be they religious, spiritual, or secular. With no conscious intent to persuade them of anything, I seek to open myself to whatever they want to convey to me. And so I expose myself not only to the great unknown of death but to its unknown impact on each person's beliefs and priorities that fall under its shadow. In a word, this book will make you privy to the dramas played out in these disquieting yet revealing moments.

One last thing which I must note before proceeding any further is the issue of confidentiality. Like congregational work, and like healthcare work in general, hospice service requires absolute confidentiality. No one else but fellow members of the hospice team such as the nurse or social worker is privy to what I say or observe about a given client. Nor is that divulged even to them unless it enables better holistic care. Thus, all the names in this narrative are pseudonyms, with no other conceivable identifying factors such as dates of the visits.

Everything else about these visits, however, is genuine. I have not, as a strikingly large number of friends and family have suggested, "enhanced" any of these tales. I have not made them more dramatic, or combined elements from one encounter with those of another. There is no need, as especially in the world of hospice, truth is not only stranger than fiction but is at least equally compelling. The only difference between this narrative and my day-to-day work is that many of the days are routine, with no particularly outstanding encounter to remark upon. On such days there are no families who wish to see a chaplain, leaving me to stop in the nursing homes to make sure the patients there are not in pain. Often these patients are asleep or minimally responsive or indifferent to the visit. On those days, the sadness of lives ebbing away just adds up, with no apparent benefit from my presence except in the occasional instance where I do see signs of pain such as moaning or rigid body posture and I report such things to the nurse.

As I was agonizing over what to call this book, and believe you me I did agonize, my husband Steve was skeptical about the first part of the title. "Encountering the edge how?" he asked. I replied, "Well, I was thinking of people like a mountain climber or an ultra-marathoner or those scientists who work real close to an active volcano." Unlike those adventurers, I do not put myself in physical danger, but I do face emotional danger. I jump into interactions that can be laced with escalating anxiety or impotent anger displaced onto me or through me onto God. But on the plus side, just like the ultra-marathoner, I undergo moments of exhilaration such as when a patient experiences spiritual healing or suddenly gains an insight into the meaning of her life. So as a hospice chaplain, I am living on the edge with its perils but also its joys. Not only that, I think using this expression about my work reveals a deeper reason for choosing it. I have taken on a challenge which forces me to see what stuff my beliefs are made of when applied to people facing suffering and death. I have taken on a dare to tear myself away from the false comfort of stock responses and to instead stand next to my clients as they totter at the boundary between the known and the unknown.

I think my personal temperament as a quiet person has a lot to do with my compatibility with this career, too. Countless patients, families, and interviewers have described my soft, low-pitched voice as soothing. I have imparted a tranquilizing presence as far back as I can remember, like the time my parents took my brother and me to see a great aunt and some other relatives in Philadelphia. That night, my brother and I were asked to decide who was going to sleep in which room with which relative—or rather, my brother, by right of seniority, did the deciding. He chose to be with the ones he deemed the more entertaining relatives, while I was relegated to my great aunt, in my young eyes a stuffy old lady. After both she and I slept well through the night, she said, "I haven't been sleeping well. But last night I slept like a baby." That was my initiation into learning I could "enter the quiet immensity of my own healing presence" (John O'Donohue).

Visiting a patient for the first time might be like how deep sea divers feel as they are about to take the plunge. I do not really know what I am going to encounter until I come face to face with the patient and the give and take between us springs into life. The information on the medical records does not tell me much. What little there is states the disease, age, ethnicity, the pain treatment plan, and includes other information such as whether there are young children in the home. As for the spiritual component, I am lucky if I get the name of their religion. Take my first visit to Lynn, for example. This patient summoned me to her home (as the family told me on her behalf) with a peculiar stipulation: that I only visit her one single time. Usually patients decide this sort of thing after, not before, meeting me, and not for very flattering reasons. The exception is when all they wish for is a prayer good for onetime use only. I figured Lynn had some unresolved question and that after she got the answer to it she was going to conserve her future remaining energy for other people. For many patients, even speaking a few words, even opening their eyes, exacts a high percentage of their available energy, much as walking for several miles would deplete mine.

Upon entering her bedroom, all curtains drawn and no lights on to compensate for the dusk-like atmosphere, a hospice volunteer named Pam was finishing up a Reiki session as Lynn reclined on a velvety brown couch. Hospice volunteers receive training over a two-month period and then a volunteer coordinator assigns each person to one or two patients. They often are drawn to this service as a way to "give back" for help they had received for loved ones on hospice some time ago. As I watched Pam's hands hover over Lynn's outstretched legs, she explained that minimizing the light in the room made Lynn feel more relaxed. I felt a calm yet alert atmosphere among the three of us.

Pam let me know that Lynn communicated just by moving one sole finger. "She used to move more of her hand, but now that is all that is left for us." Along with taking in the sadness of the implied drawn-out history of one loss after another, it was going to take a lot of intuition to figure out why Lynn wanted me there. Even if I could come again, she might not be conscious anymore or even alive. As I looked at her inquiring face, I thought about the concerns that all humans have. I thought about what every single one of us wants to know such as what our life story has amounted to. I knew that if I could guess her question and answer it, she would invest the effort to make that finger move.

As I tell you this story about Lynn, I think of Alice. B. Toklas' account that Gertrude Stein's last words to her devotees surrounding her deathbed were, "What's the answer?" When no one replied, she then queried, "In that case, what is the question?" Maybe this was Gertrude Stein's idea of having the last laugh.

But when I was with Lynn, knowing that she was aware I was a chaplain and for that reason had asked for me, I decided to ask and answer the most fundamental spiritual question there is if you get down to it: what is the meaning of life? This in part has to do with our legacy. Sensing the supremely caring atmosphere we were in, I answered, "We are here to both receive and to give love." Her hand relaxed. Her finger from the knuckle up painstakingly moved up and down as if nodding, "yes yes yes."

Chapter 1

"You're Too Nice Looking to Work for Hospice"
Being Made Welcome to My New Career

I started looking for hospice work in 2005 as I wrapped up a three-year contract with Progressive Temple Beth Ahavat Sholom in Brooklyn, New York. Though I had my share of detractors while serving there, I did have my ardent fans as well. As my contract was drawing to a close, I interviewed for pulpit as well as hospice positions, being ambivalent about leaving congregational life. The congregation was unaware that I was considering serving at a hospice. As of yet unannounced to a soul, soon after I got the offer from United Hospice of Rockland, one of these fans said, "Rabbi, I don't care how far away your next post is, I will follow you there." I told him I was overwhelmed with his faithfulness and touching sentiments, but that he would not want to fulfill his vow as the only way he would be following me would be as a hospice patient! A portrait painter would have had a heyday capturing the motley crew of emotions all over his face.

1

And that was one of the more positive reactions to my announcement of my career plans. One person made such an expression of disgust you would think I had already ritually defiled myself from contact with the dead as described in the Book of Leviticus. He was afraid I would be contaminating him in no time. Sure enough, he backed away from our remaining opportunities to get together over coffee. Someone else, upon hearing the news, raised his arms as if to protect himself, emitted an "Oh!" looked away, and retreated a step or two. Mentioning my new career to my congregants definitely was a way to throw a curveball into a conversation. (Nowadays, there is a mischievous part of me that sometimes gets a kick out of springing this surprise upon unsuspecting listeners such as fellow Bed and Breakfast guests.) Yet another congregant gave me a knowing look, saying "That is just the kind of job that would suit you." Maybe I was imagining it, having been stung by the premature end of my tenure, but it felt like the subtext of that remark was "A pulpit rabbi you should not or could not ever be." I had visited her a number of times for bereavement care, listening to her accounts of family lost in the Holocaust. Another reaction, from multiple members of the congregation, was "Oh, so you're retiring!" So onward I went, with all these votes of confidence, to life at the edge. (Though to be fair, some people greatly respect and marvel at this form of service.) And as with all new challenges, I was indeed on edge about what lay ahead.

In addition to dealing with those often skeptical responses, I was not sure how a handicap of mine would play out in this new setting. I have a listening disorder that is hard to explain and therefore hard to get people to make adjustments for. When I hear other sounds the same time that I hear speech, my brain does not allow me to ignore the extraneous sounds and focus on the speech. I hear everything, but what I hear takes some wrong turns as the brain interprets the sounds. So when I am with friends in a restaurant for example, the conversations at the other tables, the sounds of dishes being washed, the background music, and especially the sounds of coffee makers, all compete to make hearing my friends a fatiguing enterprise. This is probably what it is like for a person communicating in a second language that they do not know very well. As I discovered, nursing homes are full of noise, and sometimes the patient I was visiting spoke softly, so I did what I could to steer the patient out of the common areas and into her room or some quiet nook. (I may have what is called "Central Auditory Processing Disorder," but I never have sought a formal diagnosis.)

I had to contend with this problem from the start with my colleagues, too. If an air conditioner was rattling away at a meeting, I had to concentrate very hard to understand what they were saying. If the door was open with the copier chugging away, same effect. No matter how closely I concentrate on what people are saying on the job or off, I can guarantee you I miss a certain percentage of what is being said. More often than not, there will be some background noise which the normal brain unconsciously and automatically screens out but my brain doesn't. So if a social worker and I were standing in a hallway to discuss a patient, and I

3

heard a car going by through an open window, I would miss some of what she was saying until the sound of the car faded away.

Even when I forewarn my colleagues and friends about this listening disorder, they often forget about the problem or misunderstand it and think I am partially deaf. Moreover, my processing of speech in a noisy place takes longer, and so I confuse and annoy people with my slow reaction time. A fellow chaplain once told me that talking to me is like when a newscaster on TV says something to another one at a different location, and there is a brief delay before the latter hears what is said, and then finally responds. And so that is why I revere and seek quiet, or at least am grateful when I can hear one thing at a time, be it a conversation, a piece of music, a colleague's report, or the change in a patient's breathing from labored to relaxed and steady. I listen, and as I encounter each new patient, I wonder, like an explorer of new worlds, what unique features will come my way.

In the first weeks of my first hospice job, I had plenty to adjust to. First, I had to learn how I knew which patients to contact. At any given time, a certain number of patients are on the hospice program and they usually get there via a referral from their doctor. They have to fit criteria that more or less predict that given the usual course of the disease, the patient will live for about six months. Some of these criteria are unplanned substantial weight loss, increased sleeping, incontinence, loss of interest in life, and of course the malady itself such as cancer or heart disease. Once admitted, the patients might be living at home, in a nursing home, in an assisted living facility, or be in the middle of a hospital stay. At some hospices, they might also be in that hospice's residence. Unless a patient or family member explicitly asks the admission nurse to tell the chaplain not to contact them, my initial task is to phone them. Then if requested, within five days of admission, I visit each new patient. After the first contact, I make further visits depending on the needs and wishes of the patients and their families.

So practically the first day at my new job, I had to telephone a list of forty strangers during a crisis situation in their lives and see if they wished to have an unknown quantity like me drop by to visit for spiritual support. Meanwhile, the Christian chaplain Bruce was telephoning his forty families, as we both got hired at the same time. There we were, in a building filled with about one hundred employees, from human resources personnel to book-keepers to medical record coordinators to all those who are said to "go in the field" such as nurses, social workers, music therapists, home health aides, and of course chaplains. As I made the calls, I was relieved at how courteous the families were; I must have figured that under such an emotionally volatile situation they would have directed their anger and helplessness at me. I was so nervous that day I was glad that most of them declined my offer to visit or even call again. It was hard enough just learning how to document online; computers have to be extremely user-friendly for me to catch on quickly. For each call and visit, I had to enter what happened in their medical record, even if it were a short note like, "No chaplain desired at this time."

The main reason I was relieved not to have to make many visits initially was that I had to learn all new driving directions— starting with, as I left the building, should I turn left or right? And where was that back entrance again? In those days, I did not have a navigator, and I was more phobic about learning new directions. Some of the patients lived nearby, but government rules allow hospices to admit patients who are as far as fifty miles away from the agency building. To admit a patient more than that is not allowed because it could take too long for a member of the team to get there and give urgently needed assistance such as pain relief.

When two or more chaplains are working at the same agency, one of the tricky logistical tasks is to figure out which chaplain gets which patients. Aside from special requests for a chaplain to be of a certain religion, the main criterion for dividing up patients among chaplains is geography. But this is not easy, as of course each chaplain would like to visit patients that are either close to the agency or who live close to the chaplain's own home. My husband likes to kid that when I telephone patients who live fifty miles away, I should say, "You don't really need a chaplain today, now do you?" Traveling for visits could get very involved too, because patients can be scattered in all four directions (theoretically up to one hundred miles away from each other) and not nec- essarily be clustered near each other. On a big travelling day, I can easily log 130 miles including the commute to and from the office. The logistics can get even more complicated when one chaplain is out sick or on vacation.

At United Hospice of Rockland, when Chaplain Bruce was away for a few days, I had to assign new patients to him and to myself, call Bruce's patients to see if they wanted to see him the next week, and document the results online for his and mine. We had agreed that every other new admission would be his while I took the rest. One time, when a patient lived at that fifty-mile borderline out in Sloatsburg somewhere and was not conveniently near any of my other patients, I could not resist assigning that outlier to Bruce even though that patient should have been mine. Should I feel guilty? Maybe not, because he probably returned the favor when I was away!

The actual door-to-door travel itself that all the team had to take can be an adventure all its own. Driving, I quickly discovered, can consume more of the day (much, much more) than the visits themselves due to distance, bad weather, horrific traffic, or of course getting lost. Not only that, the risk for accidents probably ranks travel time a greater occupational hazard than the possibility of catching some disease (like the flu) making its rounds in the nursing homes. Of at least equal concern is that despite cell phones and navigators, each of us is alone in the car and therefore vulnerable to mishaps and ticklish situations, such as rude gas attendants and iffy neighborhoods. And by the time I make it all the way there, the patient may have died in the meantime. Or the patient might have changed his mind about seeing me by then or have gone to sleep for the day. Relatively rarely, the patient has not even been home, possibly because despite the call I make hours before I set out, he forgot or someone else with him did and took him on an outing. "Drat!" I say to myself among other less professional things as I trudge back to the doggone car, kicking any ill-fated debris that dares to cross my way.

My husband teases me that after a day like that that when we get rich, my chauffeur will drive me around in our Mercedes. But hospice salaries being what they are at approximately twenty-five dollars an hour, hospice pay will never be a source of wealth. I have joked with friends that I travel around like a truck driver but get paid far less. (I know this is hyperbole, as truck drivers travel considerably more than I do.)

Like anything else, such as what I happen to be wearing, I learned that the kind of car I have can be a patient's topic of choice or inspire skepticism on the part of security at gated communities. For a while, I was driving a sporty dazzling blue 1994 Mustang while my sedate Honda Civic was in for repairs. I noticed that unlike when I had my Honda, when I drove up to the gate to enter those communities, security was not so quick to wave me in. They looked askance at my hot-rod, asked for my ID, and scrutinized it at length before taking a gamble on senior safety. Once my car and I were in the grounds, a few patients pointed to the vehicle and made remarks such as, "*That's* your car? I did not expect you of all people to have a car like that." I suppose my unholy roller reduced my credibility. I never ever got remarks implying an unexpected incongruity between car and chaplain when I drove the Honda.

One of my most ridiculous and awkward driving predicaments, a perfect story for the Tappet Brothers' radio program *Car Talk*, happened as I was leaving a rest stop near Exit 8A headed northbound on the New Jersey Turnpike. Naturally, just as I had already irrevocably pulled out and had proceeded onto the highway, my nose started to bleed like its contents had to rush to an emergency exit. Fortunately I had a few tissues within clutching distance, but even so, the interval between realizing what was taking place, carefully removing one hand from the wheel at some fifty miles per hour to get at the tissues without looking at them, and at long last bringing them firmly towards my nose and holding them there, left plenty of time for me and my clothes to get an extremely red makeover.

I did not have much choice but to keep driving to the next rest stop several miles away with one hand on the wheel and one tissue-filled hand on my face. Keeping my eyes on the road con-flicted with but took first priority over keeping said nose up in the air to staunch the rosy output. I thought about pulling over to the shoulder with just one hand, but at the high speed I was travelling, such a sudden drop would have been too perilous. A race car driver I am not. I think I then put on my blinkers and anxiously yet stalwartly kept going, the next rest stop several miles away. When I got there, I was faced with the nerve-racking task of negotiating the sharply curved ramp with mostly one hand with milliseconds of intermittent help from the other. For the grand finale, I singlehandedly made an abrupt turn into a parking space. Double whew! After leaning back and pinching my nose to stop the flow, I went in to wash up. I must have looked like I had been mauled! It could have been worse. What if no tissues had been sitting on the seat or along the side pockets of the car, or as sometimes happens, all of my tissues had gone on strike and disappeared? But then again, my half-empty-glass self scolded my half-full-glass self saying, did I really have to be all by my lonesome and have this micro melodrama happen far from local roads and a good sixteen miles to the next rest area? Talk about a red-letter day.

Besides getting used to calls, driving, and visits, there were meetings to attend at the agency, such as learning the rules for functioning as part of a health care team. For example, we had to clue each other in to the patients' needs. If I saw that a patient was in pain, I was to notify the nurse. If a social worker heard a patient expressing ambivalence about their religious beliefs, she was to let me know. And I learned so much about how to wash my hands—about the most important way to avoid infection of oneself and others—I am sure I could give a twenty minute "hands on" presentation on the subject.

Another agency meeting subjected us to a detailed review of sexual harassment, complete with a hokey video of two of our own supervisors posing as coworkers with one worker "accidentally" brushing past the other. After some basic definitions, the speaker gave example after example of subtle borderline cases, such as when a male supervisor might with all innocence make comments on a female subordinate's appearance. The assumption throughout the presentation was that most sexual harassment is done by men to women. Somehow I was not too worried about my leading anyone into temptation with my feminine charms. Of all the hospice personnel in the entire agency, there were about two men in the whole lot!

I also attended meetings in the broader community such as the local board of rabbis. When I introduced myself as the new hospice chaplain in town, one rabbi (they were all or nearly all male as I recall) said, "You're with hospice? You are far too nice looking to be in hospice work." I wondered if that meant death and my legendary beauty didn't go together. I also fidgeted at what felt like a left-handed compliment. Did that imply my beauty had not opened more prestigious doors for me? But from their side, I sensed relief in the air that my being involved with hospice instead of pulpits meant that I would not be competing with them. It also meant I was no threat to the distribution of rabbinic power in that town. I knew about that sort of dynamic all too well from my pulpit work, which had power issues all of its own. The members of the board of trustees often wanted power and prestige more than spiritual fulfillment. As a pulpit rabbi, I felt like I was playing the part of a mayor who not only must maintain her own place as a leader but also constantly deal with various factions and watch her back. Those factions sometimes had conflicting, or at least different, needs and hopes. I saw that those were not the sort of circumstances that I was skilled at (a view both charitable to myself as well as to the congregation), whereas I was most effective at caring for individual congregants in crisis. Thus I switched to a career as a professional chaplain.

I can share plenty of anecdotes with you that showed me that pulpit work was not my long-term destiny. I will confine myself to two. At a temple in Parsippany, New Jersey, soon after a new temple president was elected in the middle of my first contract term, I fell out of favor. About half of the rank and file members hoped I would stay, and about half did not. Most of the board of trustees wanted me to be an "unintended" interim rabbi and not renew my contract. This in itself is par for the course in retrospect. What really shook me up though and still astounds me today is the following: after services at most temples, the congregants help themselves to refreshments and sit down at tables to socialize. At this particular temple, there was an aisle that divided the seating area in half. Someone told me that the people who wanted me to stay for another term sat on one side of that aisle, and the rest on the other, and that when someone crossed over to "the other side" there was talk. They would be asked why they were not in their own side. Once I left that temple, I was deeply saddened to hear that many friendships had foundered between people who liked me and people who did not. To suffer the results of political maneuvers as a religious leader is one thing, causing me acute spiritual distress. But the havoc it works upon the faith of the rank and file is quite another, counting as a far more grievous sin.

The second anecdote has to do with a congregation in Long Island City in Queens, New York. With no provocation that I knew of, one random day someone impersonated me on the phone and called the chairman of the board at around two o'clock in the morning. The caller said something about having to talk to him then. The chairman then woke me up soon after with a call of his own to me, infuriated to such an extent he could not completely believe me when I said I did not and of course would not ever make such a call. "Someone in the congregation sure must hate you to go to such lengths," my brother said. I never did find out who impersonated me, which by the way in the State of New York is illegal since the intent was to injure my reputation. It could be that the chairman himself made this up. If that seems implausible, how plausible is the other scenario? I chuckle at the absurdity of these two anecdotes now, but at the time, these and all the other manifestations of power plays and divisiveness constantly threw me off balance and afflicted my innermost being.

If you do not believe these stories, or you think this just happens in Jewish houses of worship, or that it just happened to me because of my own shortcomings, a May 2012 Google search revealed over 200,000 entries on clergy burnout. As one example of how extensive this problem is, a book was published with the melodramatic title, *Clergy Killers: Guidance for Clergy and Congregations under Attack*, by G. Lloyd Rediger. Interestingly, such dysfunction is not even peculiar to houses of worship. As C.P. Snow said in *The Affair*, his novel about the intricate political maneuverings of a college faculty over the ouster of one of their colleagues, one can forget "how intense and open the emotions could show in a closed society." He goes on to say: "The curious thing is, in terms of person-to-person conflict, when one moves from high affairs to the college, one moves from a more sheltered life to a less." And so the lack of protection from my proponents and the distress I suffered in pulpit life was not even about religion, but about fundamental human behavior in any small lasting informal society.

In comparison with the emotionally wrenching years in pulpit work, the adjustments I have had to make to chaplaincy have been kids' stuff. As you will see in the story below, not only did I adapt to serving people who were not Jewish, but also found my way to nourishing their spiritual needs.

One of my very first visits as a hospice chaplain was to Judy, who was the matriarch of her family. She was an African American who was just hours from the end and unable to speak. Her husband and other loved ones were quietly arrayed near her bed or sitting gingerly on it in an expansive bedroom. As her daughter gestured for me to sit on the edge of the bed, I glanced around their upscale home and thought about how the beauty of their surroundings seemed to mock the ugliness of what they were going through. They had asked me to pray, and I offered generically spiritual words from the heart, trying to unobtrusively avoid the "J" word so I would not falsely express something contrary to my beliefs. What I often say in such cases is something like, "May your loved one feel God's nearness. God's love is all around us, surrounding us. Judy, this love is going from your head to your feet, God is your protector who neither slumbers nor sleeps and you will be welcomed in God's embrace. We give thanks for the love that this family has given and received."

There was a reverent mood, and Judy's daughter joyfully said, "We are so comforted to have a Christian presence at this time." This is one of many "amusing" situations I would bring home to hubby to enliven dinner. Of course, how I handle my identity is a serious matter for each family. In this particular case I deemed it more important that the family felt comforted than intellectually enlightened as to who I "really" was. I was already different enough being white, and I did not wish to throw my differences into even sharper relief. I hoped I was serving them at the more universal level of a human offering ministry. One of the draws of being a chaplain is the potential to transcend racial, religious, ethnic, and other boundaries, which can all shrink to insignificance in the face of impending death. While I am not a Christian clergyperson, to that family I was ushering in God's love and care within a familiar and therefore comforting framework: that of a "standard issue" chaplain. Of course, if they had asked me to officiate at the funeral or had become puzzled by my Jesus-free prayer, I would have had to gently explain that I was Jewish and see if they would have preferred the services of the Christian chaplain on the team for future contact.

My Christian counterpart has his own challenges when it comes to interfaith work. I remember a colleague telling me, "When I pray with a Jewish patient, and I don't end the prayer with an 'in Jesus' name, Amen,' I feel like I am writing an email without pushing the 'send' button." To which another colleague retorted, "That may be, but to the Jewish patient, as soon as they hear 'Jesus' then that's like hitting the 'delete' button!"

All in all though, the interfaith nature of my work often enables all parties to push past religious barriers and to resonate with the spiritual values virtually all religions share. Take for example a situation where the patient was dying of AIDS. His son John was in jail and though the prison did not even allow him to visit his father on his deathbed, I knew that with chaplain-to-chaplain contact, there was a good chance that he would be allowed to make a telephone call that same day to his father. The prison chaplain I contacted happened to be Muslim. So there we were Muslim and Jew, collaborating on behalf of a Baptist patient. I never did find out if the call came to pass. As is often the case in hospice care, carrying out such actions depends on many factors, in this case the prison warden, the nursing home staffer who first answered the phone, and whether the patient was awake at the time. Chaplaincy unites not only religions, but groups within religions. When I attend the National Association of Jewish Chaplains' annual conference, the differences among Orthodox, Conservative, and Reform Jews do not matter a jot.

I owe my comfort and even fascination with diverse cultures to my upbringing. My parents were very open to receiving visitors from other countries and other ethnic groups. I remember the time my parents' Russian friends brought along friends from their church choir between Christmas and New Year's. They sang some folk tunes for us and conversed amongst themselves in Russian. I remember too how my mother inadvertently frightened them when she asked them to mail a letter for her after they left. They did not do so, perhaps fearing that the letter had to do with notifying the authorities about them because they carried many bad memories from Russia about the KGB. Other visitors I remember included a biracial couple, very unusual in the nineteen-sixties, especially in a small city like Erie, Pennsylvania.

I became interested enough in other cultures to become a foreigner myself. I attended a semester-abroad program in college. While living for one summer in Puerto de la Libertad, El Salvador, and then for one semester in the cities of Bogotá and Silvia in Colombia, I felt the freedom and stimulation of being in places with different norms than where I was raised. It fascinated me to experience wearing ponchos, to lunch on huge papayas and luscious soft mangos, and to witness celebrations for the communal construction of indigenous homes. I also was exposed to new attitudes toward time (more laid back), religion (more loosely defined), and money (far scarcer). As I learned about the Hispanic and indigenous cultures as well as the Spanish language, I felt like I was in an alternate reality.

Visiting with patients, particularly the first time, is something like a sojourn in a foreign country too. I have to learn the language of their assumptions as formed by their life history, their lingo as shaped by their religious heritage, and their private secret code as they encounter the edge of the beyond. My job is to enter their rapidly shifting terrain to help them make sense of their past, present, and future. In the coming chapters, I invite you to explore more of these foreign places with me in this sometimes disturbing, sometimes uplifting, and sometimes surprising journey.

Chapter 2

"WHAT DO YOU DO WITH A DRUNKEN SAILOR?"
From the Singing Chaplain's Repertoire

As you accompany me to my patients, you may find yourself throwing various assumptions overboard. Such as when I sing to them, you might think I only sing sweet and religious songs like "Swing Low Sweet Chariot," or "Kumbaya, My Lord," or something based on the Psalms such as "May the Words of My Mouth." Sam, twenty-eight years old and formerly a policeman, was one of the youngest residents in a nursing home relatively near my office; he was there on account of a disease that was stealthily stealing his motor abilities. Almost every time I stopped in, he gave me a broad delighted smile. But he decidedly did not want to hear a "girlie" thing like a hymn, though his mother did. She visited him at the nursing home practically every day to patiently feed him lunch served along with her cheery and loving talk. I often saw her during my weekly visits, and because she found my hymns soothing, I sang them for her benefit when she was around. She kept requesting them every time our visits coincided, although she had a thing or two to say to God due to the disease that was destroying her son. Sam, as I implied before, was not ambivalent about religion. He simply was not on board with it, so I tried to think of something nonreligious to sing. I had recently found out that one of the things Sam missed a lot at the nursing home was beer. Since I could not quickly arrange to have it made available (this would have required a doctor's order), I thought a song about such beverages might raise his spirits at least in part. So I energetically sang "What Do You Do with a Drunken Sailor," "Ninety-Nine Bottles of Beer," and "In Heaven There Is No Beer." All of these elicited his distinctive lingering smile. On subsequent visits, when I asked if he wanted to hear these again, he formed an even longer-lasting smile and said, "Sure!" Even his mom allowed herself a grin. At later visits when he could no longer indicate what he wanted to hear, his smile acted as confirmation.

One of Sam's dying wishes was to get a tattoo showing his police rank and years of service. Given his condition, the procedure would have been painful, but his response was, in his soft high-pitched voice, "I'm tough." Unfortunately, this was complicated to arrange. For one thing, he was not strong enough to leave the nursing home to appear at the tattoo parlor. There was some talk of getting a tattoo artist to make a house call, but by then, Sam was too weak to endure getting the tattoo. Soon after his disease had progressed to that stage, my husband Steve and I saw a performance of Hawaiian hula dancers, and I noticed that they had tattoos—not the kind we typically think of with pictures of hearts and arrows and letters, but of geometric shapes. One of the Hawaiian performers explained that their tattoos signify such matters as family connections and position in the social hierarchy. The higher the rank, the more elaborate and more numerous the designs. I thought of Sam, who wanted us to read his epitaph on his skin, proclaiming who he was and what he had achieved.

As he got weaker, more and more family members dropped by to offer their physical presence if nothing else, and to be there for each other. By then Sam was virtually nonverbal. At one of my last visits, a friend around his age and his dad Tim were there, trying to coax him into nibbling at a peanut butter and jelly sandwich. They did not get very far in promoting the idea. I asked Tim how Halloween had gone the week before, just to find an excuse to stay for a little while and share a few moments with the other visitors. Tim was glad to have something to do like chitchat with me besides stare at Sam lying there so listlessly and quietly. He launched into great detail of how he and his fiancée celebrated the holiday. (Another layer of sadness in this story is that Sam's mom and Tim were divorced. They even made an elaborate schedule to make sure they did not visit Sam at the same time.) He took out his smartphone and showed me various pictures of how they had decorated the house with the requisite bats and spiders and of their outdoor display of goblins and their spooky peers. But the real horror was Sam, sprawled out on the bed like a forgotten doll, ghastly, with his eyes wide open and unblinking. We were caught in the eerie moment of his being present to us less and less, and the family and I deepening our connections with each other more and more.

Before he died, I saw him one more time, and we were alone. As I held his hand I felt the impulse to thank him for his years of service as a police officer, and I like to think that what I said registered in his consciousness because he squeezed my hand at one point. But I will never know for sure. There was one more task to do: a journal for visitors lay open on the bureau. Next to the messages left for each other by home health aides and by each parent to the other such as "Sam slept peacefully after I bathed him," I left a message telling his mother and father my final words to their son, hoping that would be of some comfort. I thought about the fact that each parent was not in the company of the other each time the entries in this journal were read. And after Sam's death, would it be discarded as too painful a reminder and meet its own premature end, or would it be saved and cherished by one of them as a record of their last ties to their son, and if so, by whom?

In hospice work, connections usually must be made quickly, as there is often not much time to play with. You literally do not know if a visit will turn out to be the last, even if the patient does want you to return. And so social preliminaries get telescoped or omitted altogether. Once made, connections can deepen so rapidly it is like speeding up a film and jumping months ahead. In minutes of meeting a family member, he can be telling me concerns that only his closest friends had been privy to. Or I could be the only person on earth he has ever unveiled those concerns to. The situation itself is rife with intensity, but the mere presence of a chaplain causes tension to build. My being there, not even to pray but simply to listen, is often all it takes for most patients to unleash a prolonged rainfall of words. Once the downpour begins, there is no joining it with even a sprinkle of words of my own, a truth confirmed the times I have been foolish or anxious enough to try and do so. Then after I hear a person out, singing is one skill at my disposal that contributes to the creation and maintenance of comfort and trust and mutual pleasure. The songs not only do not have to be religious, they can be downright irreverent, as was evident in the example with Sam.

Another family where nontraditional song fit best was with the Witfields. Originally, I met them as I made my rounds of my new patients in the skilled nursing home section of a senior care center. I saw them about once a month for almost a year. Mrs. Witfield, the one on hospice, shared the same room with her husband, but they each slept in separate beds like roommates. One of the nicer rooms in the nursing wing, there was a couch to the left of the door and plenty of space for a stately mahogany bureau topped off with model airplanes and a picture of Mr. Witfield in a pilot's uniform. Both had served as pilots in World War II. He lived there not only to be with her, but because he needed care himself for severe short-term memory problems.

Every time I came in, I had to go through the same ritual of Mr. Witfield's questions because on some level I was a brand new face: "Where do you live? What religion are you? Where does your husband serve?" Often he was mentally located in the past around World War II, and he would ask if I were a pilot too. I would always roll my eyes at that and say being a passenger was more than enough for me when it came to flying. He always gave a hearty laugh at that. And when I said I was a "chaplain," he must have thought I meant a military chaplain. I think it puzzled him when I said my husband was a civilian, and there I was, a chaplain with a peculiar gender. He always informed me that both he and his wife were pilots and that she was a WAC. So naturally I sang out, "The WACs and the WAVES are winning the war, parlez-vous," and they rewarded me with amused laughter. Even though the repetition of all this at each visit was annoying, I tried to think of it as a ritual worth going through that let me bask in their delight with the sheer pleasure of connecting with another friendly soul.

To see what concerns they might have, I needed to move the conversation forward each time I visited in order not to be in a time loop like the weatherman Phil Connors played by Bill Murray in *Groundhog Day*. So I had to slip in comments and questions that pushed the conversation into new channels. One time I interrupted with, "How long does it take to fuel a plane?" (I think he said about four hours, depending on the kind of plane.) This deepened our connection a bit as he liked the fact that I was interested in his career. This deepening became far more important, and a far greater challenge, when his wife truly started going downhill in a big way. They were very close, and he was reluctant to step out of their room when she was feeling too sick to come along. His routine had been to walk behind while pushing her along in her wheelchair. It was a wonder, in this limited environment, to see their love thrive, as plants and animals do in the most unlikely and inhospitable places such as deserts and in the sunless depths of the ocean. I was apprehensive about his memory loss though, wondering how I would ever help him anticipate the great loss looming ahead as he learned of his wife's condition again and again. How would I ever help him start to grieve? And how would he be able to bear it?

I decided on my next visit to do two things: to enter the room and talk in a serious and somewhat sad tone from start to finish. I said how sorry I was that Mrs. Witfield felt so sick. I asked about how they had met, and so on, and how he felt at that moment. By then, my efforts were unnecessary. He seemed to have found his own way of coping, which was to exist emotionally even further back in time, ever further from the menacing present. He talked with me about applying to be in the Army, and his work with RCA. He even offered to help me get a job there. (It was defunct in the 1980s.) As usual, he was very jolly ensconced in the good old days. Then a strange thing happened a week or two later. Mrs. Witfield seemed to be getting better, not worse, and finally the hospice team evaluated her as doing well enough to come off of hospice. She indeed came off but sadly, after being on hospice for months upon months, she practically died overnight. I am not sure how much Mr. Whitfield understood about that. When I saw him shortly after her death, he seemed to think she was away at the hospital. When I saw him on subsequent visits, he did not refer to her at all or respond when I brought up the subject. Perhaps he had found some sort of refuge in one of his replays of earlier days, or was caught in the relatively recent episode when he thought she was only temporarily away, recuperating in a hospital. I hope whatever "groundhog day" he is stuck in will continue to be one of the pleasanter days of his life, maybe when "the WACs and the WAVES were winning the war."

I do not go out of the way to introduce avant-garde modes of singing, so most of the time my selections consist of hymns or chants, or for the nonreligious, American folk and patriotic tunes such as Pete Seeger's "If I Had a Hammer" and Samuel Francis Smith's "My Country, 'Tis of Thee." This is where the heart-warming anecdotes pour in. One smartly dressed patient in his late eighties, relaxing in his living room with a self-effacing demeanor, remarked "I've never been sung to before." He did not know quite what to expect from a chaplain, but I wager that a solo singing performance was not among his guesses. I said, "I guess in the old days only royalty could get their own personal concert. Now more of us can." After I finished singing "Home on the Range," this modest gentleman and I sat there and chatted about this or that trifle, which temporarily whisked him away from illness and anxiety. I call such a result of small talk or singing a "respite visit," meaning relief from what loomed ahead as I just described. You can live in the moment, no matter how close that moment is to the very last one.

Another lovely thing that happens every so often with music is when the patients whom I see join in on their favorite hymns, singing or simply mouthing the words along with me, even when it takes them considerable effort. Or family members will sing along, harmonizing with me, forming an instant if transient choral backdrop.

This happened when I made a visit to an extremely devout Catholic family taking care of Mary in her apartment complex off a short side street. She was close to turning one hundred and was very lucid. She lay in a hospital bed alongside the living room bay windows while her two daughters and I gathered round to pray with her. Mary's home was swamped with ornate crosses, pictures of the Pope and other religious figures, as well as Christmas decorations that everyone wanted to postpone removing as long after Christmas as possible. The decorations echoed the hopeful and appreciative attitude of the family and of the numerous visitors coming and going. After praying, I suggested various hymns I could sing, and Mary felt like I was transporting her to church, which she missed dearly. With the two daughters spontaneously joining in and adding a few more verses that I either did not know or I felt were "too Christian" for me to sing, the singing reinforced the sacred atmosphere. As they harmonized with me, we created a miniature choir. "If you cannot go to church, then we'll bring the church to you," I said. Her hope was to live through the twelve days of Christmas and join her Savior shortly thereafter. She did indeed die about a month into the new year.

One other touching musical event I recall is of my visits to the Jewish Orthodox patient Jacob and his buoyant Slavic health aid Veera who lived in Monroe Township. Jacob used to go to services, so from my first visit on, I sat beside him and chanted and sang some of the basic prayers of the service for him, with the separation of men and women for prayer no longer operational. For some patients, as they age, the outward signs of religion become irrelevant, leaving the core essences such as expressing love and reverence toward God through prayer. He liked hearing the prayers and joining in very much, and after Veera rushed to clamp a yarmulke on Jacob's head, she produced her iPhone and videotaped my on-screen cantorial debut. The upshot of my media appearance is that at my next visit, Veera told me that Jacob watched the video of my little service every day I was not there, enabling him to pray daily as he used to do. Not only that, Veera reported that Jacob's son was pleased with the prayer-on-demand video, too.

When I make my rounds, sometimes the point is not for me to sing at all when I come on the scene, but to elicit it from others and draw out their own creative sparks. On my way in to a facility to make some visits, I noticed a resident standing expectantly near the nursing station, his radar out for a potential audience. I know the feeling of hoping for an audience for my own creative outlets, so I obliged even though he was not one of my patients. I think too that particular day I was longing to interact with someone who could be more communicative, as most of the nursing home patients under my care had so few means left for connecting with me, and the nursing staff were often too busy or too jaded by their work to stop and chat. This resident, ignored by everyone else in the vicinity, was humming and humming, so I asked him what the melody was. He told me it was his own song. He then removed his Bowler hat, and displayed his original large print lyrics lodged in the rim, protected by a band of trusty plastic. I asked for a performance and he did not need any coaxing to do so. It was a corny but lilting rhyming song about a woman who always won in alimony cases. More likely than not, he had drawn on ample personal experience for his theme. During future visits to this particular facility, I do not know what became of him, as I never saw him hovering near the nursing station again.

Singing, whether done by me or someone else, almost always brings comfort, warmth, relaxation, respite from thinking about heavy issues, or even renewed energy. But I can remember one time where offering song turned out to be a very bad idea. When I see patients who are nonverbal, I try to communicate by singing to see if they might respond by opening their eyes, smiling, and so on. If I see any signs that they would rather have quiet, such as by turning their head away or firmly closing their eyes, I of course stop. I have so little to go on when no one is around who knows their past that when my intuition fails, I simply try gently singing in a low pitch to see if it is welcome. One time, as I was softly singing a hymn to a nonverbal bedbound patient wearing a highly visible cross around her neck, she slowly started to rise into a rigid sitting position, staring wide-eyed directly ahead, her cross sliding off center. Maybe she thought she heard the angels singing and that God was coming for her. I stopped, and she soon lay back down, her cross once again centered and at peace on her chest. Whew! In that case, holding her hand might have been the better option, but I did not want to risk giving her any more unintended signals. I murmured some pleasant words and beat my retreat. That was my first and last visit with her. Maybe she knew she was in her final days and even final hours after all, and was telling me her chaplain a lot more than I thought I was inadvertently telling her.

Music from other sources than personal singing does not necessarily guarantee spiritual or any other kind of wellbeing either. In an effort to perk up the acoustically and otherwise barren atmosphere of nursing homes, the staff will sometimes pipe background music into the hallways. This usually consists of the pop tunes the residents or their visiting children had heard in their youth. I had been visiting a bedbound but alert gentleman named Albert whose main theme every visit was the lousy and indifferent care he received. He had inspirational messages posted all over the otherwise minimalist room, and various nauseatingly cute drawings (made by volunteers?) adorning what space was left. He often gestured to a stack of religious pamphlets fanned out on his bedside table and pressed me to take one. During one visit, as he was reminiscing over his career as a truck driver, we heard "Hotel California" playing in the background. I myself have taken the lyrics to mean that the hotel guest is in some kind of hell after his life is over, at the hotel where "you can check out any time you like, but you can never leave." Albert had another interpretation, which captured a hell of a different nature: "That guy's like me. I'm never gonna get outta here." Unwittingly, this song only served to remind him of how his disease had imprisoned him and put him at the mercy of "these people here who don't care." He knew perfectly well that the only exit from his "hotel" would be via the Grim Reaper, who did not tarry overly long.

Aside from such a heart-rending reaction to piped-in music, a more benign problem with it overall is that it can amount to too much of a good thing; the novelty wears off (even for me as a visitor) and it comes to be just another unsolicited sound to block out of consciousness. Moreover, it cuts into the time some people prefer for quiet. Nursing homes are noisy: beepers go off on residents when they lean too far from their wheelchair and might fall; residents sound off to themselves, or to each other or to the world at large; announcements on the paging system blare so loudly I sometimes jump; and oxygen tanks make percussive noises rivaling a rock band drummer that add to the din. Thus quiet, O blessed quiet, is a premium commodity. As with other areas in our lives, we need a balance when it comes to music or other sounds; part of my job is to judge whether I should sing or not, and if I do, whether the singing should be religious or secular, energizing or soothing.

There are many other decisions besides musical ones I have to make on the spot as I observe what patients say and how they say it, and I glean what I can from their tone of contentment, enthusiasm, displeasure, anxiety, impatience, curiosity, or indifference. I also take note of how they move around, what they look like, what their home looks like, and who else is present. On top of that, if this is after the first visit, I think about what took place at the previous visit and how that might guide my plan for offering care. One of the complicated interpersonal dynamics I have to assess is how patients and their families view me. Do they see me as an authority figure ready to levy guilt for their religious failings?

Do they see me as a sweet little angel they can pour out their soul to without reservations? What ambivalence might they feel about inviting a chaplain over? No matter what they are thinking, part of my task is to minimize anything about me that could inhibit what they need to share with me or their expression of what they would like me to do.

Overall, offering my own singing is like bringing homemade cookies or a homemade greeting card; I am sharing something of myself and making myself vulnerable to their reactions. Will they like the cookies? My voice? Such sharing can dial down a patient's hesitation to share of herself in turn.

Chapter 3

"RABBI, YOU HAVE A FLAT TIRE!"
When the Chaplain Is Not in Charge

Even in the context of nearing the end of life, the patient and I have to sort out the nature of the relationship between us, no matter how transient it may turn out to be. Part of that relationship is the power imbalance between me as the professional and the patient. The patients are much more vulnerable than I, often at the mercy of others to be moved or fed. Beyond that of course they, or at least their families, are consciously confronting death. I on the other hand am perceived as crisis-free, physically strong, more sure in my religious beliefs and of course healthy. (Note I said "perceived as.") Also, as with any clergy, people tend to see me as an authority figure for good or for ill. I do what I can to mitigate this unequal footing by asking if they wish to have a visit from me in the first place. Some patients who perhaps have not made any decisions for themselves all day may regain some of their dignity by asking me to leave the room and come back another day, if at all. If I am invited to stay, I offer them choices as to what we might do, such as converse, pray, sing, play a game such as Scrabble, or just quietly be with each other. Even so, it is tricky to offer help without the patient feeling inferior, patronized, or even more powerless or humiliated. Or they may feel obligated to "say the right thing" about their beliefs in front of clergy. In fact the word "help" is itself demeaning, and so I say in my introductory remarks, "Can I be of any service to you?" Thus I try to approach them as humbly as possible.

I got this idea of using the word "service" instead of "be of help" from Dr. Rachel Naomi Remen, a doctor who writes about spiritual approaches to the medical world. She says: "When you help, you see life as weak. When you fix, you see life as broken. When you serve, you see life as whole." I sent this quote in an email to the whole hospice team, as once a week I send a "spiritual quote of the week" for a bit of uplift and welcome relief from the strictly work-related emails we all get.

Every so often, a patient will momentarily turn around our relationship by making me the more vulnerable one, or making me the one being helped or even spiritually enlightened. If you are reading this book to see if you want to be a hospice chaplain, and you are interested in being in charge, then this job would not be for you. I am very glad when the patient can take charge, because it can raise her self-worth and sense of meaning.

Miss Betty was an ardently devout Baptist recently confined to her bed in the same nursing home that had "Hotel California" playing in the background. She was a favorite among the staff because of her devotion and exuberant personality. All you had to do after a bad day was go see Miss Betty and you would feel refreshed. It was a great blow to staff when she was admitted to hospice. They at first resisted the fact that she could no longer amble along the halls and had become bedbound. However, she still was very enthusiastic about having anyone come in who was interested in prayer and eagerly beckoned them to enter her room. She took the lead when I asked whether she preferred to hear me pray or have me listen to her do the praying. I usually do not even mention the latter choice, but I had a hunch she might take me up on it, and she did. First, she started to recite the "Our Father," and I almost stopped paying attention to her exact words, figuring she was just going to trot through the entire prayer. But then I saw that midway into it she had segued into spontaneous prayer and included me in it. After thanking God for bringing me to her, she then asked God to provide me comfort and peace. I thanked her for invoking God's blessing, murmuring that usually I am the one who does that for others. Betty smiled knowingly. I also told her that I was comforted by her asking God to bless me, and it was true. Having to almost always build up the other person's strength can sap my own, and so the occasional boost from the other direction replenishes my own stores.

The patients themselves on occasion do all they can to preserve their own dignity and independence. Their wealth, too, can cut into the power imbalance, giving them a sense of more options to consider. They can, for example, employ higher quality help for longer periods of time, and have more material comforts like a fine home with a gorgeous view, and more emotional comforts like knowing their children will be well provided for. One of these wealthier patients was Marilyn, related to a former government leader and who lived in a log cabin the family built by themselves. I saw a photograph of her and an American president on the wall by the entrance, signed by him. The former winery Marilyn's family had owned had been on the property, but all physical evidence of it was gone except for a wooden sign in back of the cabin with indistinct letters which were well on the way to perishing given enough snow and rain and baking hot sun. Nothing was there now in the back except unruly grasses. How I loved going over to the cabin; every wall, floor, countertop, and table were made of burnished wood, looking amber-colored when the sun enhanced it like deftly applied makeup. I was most taken with a spiral staircase, also of wood, that led from the living room to the patient's bedroom.

During our first visit, she gave me a memoir she had written about taking a substantial monetary gift and using it all to get a boat, hire a crew, and tour Greece for one summer. As weak as she was, she even signed the book for me. I felt moved as I might have been one of the last recipients of her autograph. But what surprised me much more is that when she said, "It's time for me to rest now," she did not stay on the first floor. Without help from the aide, she methodically went step by step, on and on up the tightly winding spiral staircase, and at last having conquered the obstacle, made it to her bed. The aide agreed it was very uncomfortable, but that this routine made Marilyn happy. Although the mantra in hospice work is to reduce pain, as with everything else, there are exceptions and tradeoffs. She found comfort from an activity that indicated she was very much alive and still "in the game." Perhaps it counterbalanced the mounting indignities that assaulted her as she deteriorated day by day. Electing to endure pain can mean retaining power.

In addition to a patient's own efforts, a way for me to voluntarily mitigate the power imbalance is to let my patients be the ones who initiate personal questions. The very act of asking a question puts the questioner in the driver's seat, allowing him to take control of the dialogue. More importantly, getting personal information helps him feel connected with me. I freely answer unless I feel the question is unduly personal or that the truth about my life might upset patients. Their most common initial questions are, "What church do you belong to?" "Are you married?" "Do you have children?" "How can you do this work?" and non-rhetorical ones like "There is nothing like a mother's love, is there?" When I say, "I'm Jewish", the most popular response from Christians has been, "That's all right with me; we're children of the same God." Somehow such comments about my being Jewish as being "all right" smacks of a smidgen of prejudice on their part, as when I hear Christians say, "Some of my best friends are Jewish."

Concerning the question as to whether I have children, I always like to have a little fun with that, and I respond with, "Not last time I checked." This gets a chuckle and avoids the awkward silence that would often otherwise inevitably ensue. Bad enough that I am a Jew; not having children puts me even more at the fringes of the norm. As for a mother's love coming in first place, well, let us just say concerning my own mother that precious little mothering made it through the convolutions of her mental illness. So answering the question literally about my own mother's love would not exactly be comforting to the patient. I mean, I had the kind of mother who for sport guessed when various people we knew would die. So I just smile and nod, dreaming what it would have been like to have had such a mother as the patient's. As for how I can do this work, these anecdotes speak for themselves. I usually answer that being able to connect with them and be with all kinds of people is very rewarding.

A very different illustration of a patient taking the upper hand is for that patient to come off of hospice alive and to be aware of it. Mr. Lin comes to mind, a Chinese gentleman who "graduated" from hospice (the informal lingo we use for making it off alive) not once but two times. All of his life he had beat the odds against surviving, including his role in World War II. When Mr. Lin first came onto hospice, I found him working in his backyard garden, which was but one tiny sample of all the adjoining farmland he owned. He contentedly showed me the various vegetables he was tending, and pooh-poohed the nurse's admonition that he should not overexert himself. Finding a hospice patient outside, let alone engaged in physical action, was a novelty. Meanwhile, an intimidatingly abundant collection of cats, which almost crossed the line to being an infestation of them, were lolling about on the grass. Naturally they frequented Mr. Lin's property because he could not resist the pleasure of seeing the felines indulge in his culinary giveaways.

The next time I came to see Mr. Lin, the cool day favored going indoors. There I found an even more abundant and even more over-whelming collection: a phalanx of blue and white Chinese vases spanning from the innocuously small to the grotesquely large. They hogged the floor, dominated all available table tops, lined the halls, and practically did all but invade the bathroom. When-ever our conversation lagged, all I had to do was point to a few vases, and he would unravel a story connected with where they came from or how he came to buy them. He would explain how high a level of quality they had. "If they are smooth, then they are of the highest quality," he informed me as he had me touch one to see for myself. "And they must be blue and white. If you see other colors on them, that's just for tourists," he said with displeasure. Moving on to a more personal matter, he mentioned that when his wife was alive, "she complained about my having so many vases all over the house." I then made my own move to personal statements: "Well, my husband and I are the same way. He loves to save everything and I find the house too crowded." How Mr. Lin felt about his vases has given me more understanding about my husband's feelings of the larger-than-average quantity of items we own that he labels as having "sentimental value."

Over the course of a year Mr. Lin always had something new to talk about. Once I saw some martial arts on his television. As soon as I commented on that, he showed me how I might save my life by using some martial art techniques. He said if someone jumped on my back, rather than lean back in an attempt to throw him off, that I should lean forward, continuing the motion my opponent started. I'll have to keep that in mind! When there was no outside stimulus to conversation, such as the vases or the television, he frequently told me with pride about his narrow escapes in World War II aboard ship. These escapes were from both disease and from enemy fire. He also proudly mentioned how later in life he defeated death despite various other maladies. He won over death again when he graduated from hospice over a year after he signed on. He then came on yet again for several months, and emerged victorious once more in his battle against death. When I left Princeton Hospice about a year after that, he still had not come back on. For all I know, he could still be triumphantly negotiating with antique dealers for new collectibles to add to his blue and white retinue.

Upsetting the power imbalance works well when I am the one letting it happen. But there are less benign situations where someone else on hand other than the patient and family tries to take on the role of providing spiritual support in a dominating way. Not only do such persons usurp my role, they are, as faux chaplains, engaging in just the opposite of what clinically trained chaplains do. That is, despite best intentions, some people actually are preying on rather than praying for the patient and/or family, thus using the power imbalance for ill.

The problem of this misuse may be most clear in a context outside of hospice. A few weeks or so after the horrors of 9/11, victims' families gathered in the renovated Central Railroad

Terminal in Liberty State Park in Jersey City. A slew of social services were there to provide comfort to them in various ways, including a meal and the chance to pick up urns for their loved one's ashes. Chaplain organizations, including the Association of Professional Chaplains (Protestant) and the National Association of Jewish Chaplains, had summoned their members to help out with this event and circulate among the families to offer their nonjudgmental listening ears. I spent my time listening to families vent their anger and shock and feeling of senselessness. What I found most appalling was that some of the religious people on hand not trained to be chaplains were viewing the families as ripe for "being ready to know the Lord." They handed out pamphlets galore and delivered their message but did not lend their ears. Yes, when people are in crisis they may find meaning and support by belief in a caring God. But people in crisis are vulnerable, and have less capacity to make decisions, including theological ones. A crisis can heighten ambivalence toward religion as well as resolve it. As for the goal to save more souls, I have grave ethical objections to an "ends justifies the means" approach. I protest the promotion of religion in general and/or a specific religion in particular when people are hurting. It is the height of disrespect and an attempt at mind control in my view. In short, I consider this to be spiritual scamming.

Back to hospice, this same problem of an unsolicited dosing of religion happened with a fellow named Bob. Along with his wife Jill, I would see him in his upper-middle-class home, often resting in a bed which dominated the living room, watching an old movie on his generously-sized television stationed near the foot of his bed. The bedrooms were upstairs, and the bed was moved downstairs so there would be no need to transport him from one floor to another. During my second visit, his wife was there as usual, but this time she was with a friend Anna she had told me about who was "very religious." Uh-oh. Jill jubilantly informed me that "yesterday she prayed with us for a whole hour." Now you might think that such news would be a chaplain's dream, but that is not the truth at all. A red flag went right up! Part of my job is to get at the deeper levels of what is really going on in terms of how religion might camouflage or cloak other concerns.

Jill urged me to go over to Bob and sing some hymns, because the first time I visited, he hummed a few along with me in his resonant emphatic voice. As I approached the bed, with Anna and Jill forming a backdrop, I was thinking about that one-hour prayer session, and how such a lengthy interaction of any kind, religious or not, would have severely taxed his powers of concentration. At that first visit of mine, I quickly observed that about ten minutes of interaction was all he could tolerate. After that upper limit, he needed some quiet, which is quite common with persons at that time of life. So I thought despite the wife's urging and Bob's fine unison singing, that I should offer him a choice between hymns and nonreligious music or even none at all, and sure enough he went for the secular option. Not only that, he said his top choice would have been country music, but regrettably I had to tell him I did not have that genre in my paltry repertoire.

But you may well ask, what was going on when he sang along with my hymns during my first visit? Since he had dementia, just hearing a well-known melody of any kind might have triggered his response. Or it could have been he wanted to please his wife Jill, as religion seemed to be much more of a comfort to her than to him. Or maybe he was trying to please me, the chaplain. Or maybe that time but not the subsequent time, he did want to connect with God. (See how complicated religion can become?) But come to think of it, he expressed ambivalence even then via a critique of my in-house performance: after I had concluded some spirituals he said, "That was fine. But don't make that your day job. And besides, you have grey in your hair." (It is very common, by the way, for persons with dementia to be uninhibited and tell it like it is.) The irony here, of course, is that I have made singing part of my day job. I am not sure why he had to add the discouraging part about my gray hair; maybe he was indulging in a bit of schadenfreude, trying to level the playing field of our relative misfortunes. That was his own bid in shifting the power imbalance between care giver and care receiver.

The plot thickened when Jill's devout friend came over that second time I was there. She immediately launched into extensive preaching to Jill and me about how prayer heals. She was so insistent I felt cornered and trod upon. Just think how any patient ambivalent towards religion would feel under those circumstances. I felt frustrated because I think prayer should be about coping with reality, not indulging a fantasy. I resent any theology that implies God helps some people (who presumably are not spiritually superior) over others. I get really steamed when people say, God rescued so-and-so from a disaster like Hurricane Katrina, 9/11, or a school shooting. I cannot countenance this folk theology because everyone forgets that means God did not rescue the vast majority of those hapless guys who did not make it, let alone prevent the tragedy from hitting a populated area in the first place. If God could intervene for some people, then why not for others, or better yet, why not for everyone? There has to be some way of thinking about God besides being a rescuer or not being one. If I survived a hurricane, or beat the odds to live much longer than forecasted, I could not then conclude that God was my salvation, because it would mean God cruelly or at least capriciously was not the savior for all those other equally deserving souls.

Extensive silence, not talk, is the hallmark of a professional spiritual caregiver and this faux chaplain was not letting Jill's voice be heard. Anna then approached the bed to continue her sermon. Given Bob's rejection of religious singing, I felt he was literally a captive audience, bedbound unless moved by a caregiver to a wheelchair. As Jill's friend urged me to sing hymns to him, I had to firmly say that Bob did not wish to hear them. She did not insist, but continued to tell Jill about prayer and examples of how it performed healing.

I was concerned about what she was implying about the patient's chances for survival because once someone enrolls on hospice, the family knows that we are talking about the last half year or so of a person's life given the usual course of the disease. The conflict I felt was that her friend was confusing the issue.

No matter how well intentioned, this could make Jill's grieving even more painful: "Why didn't the prayers work?" she might lament when the time came to mourn. "Why didn't God hear me?" Added to the death itself could be the spiritual pain of a God who did not deliver or even worse, had spurned her as unworthy. At the moment of my visit, the spouse and especially the patient were under duress, and so I felt duty bound to speak up and say to Anna, as golden as her intentions might have been, "I hear your examples of how prayer can heal. But you may be raising false hopes, because sometimes bad things happen even when we pray they not happen." She murmured agreement, but I am sure she did not appreciate this nuancing of her message. I imagine she was probably quite taken aback, given that I was introduced as a "religious" person.

A chaplain's lot is not always a straightforward one. I felt awkward in this case, jockeying for the position of taking the lead in pastoral care. It did feel strange advocating for less—not more—prayer. Moreover, I was taking the chance that I was depriving the spouse of a short-term source of comfort. Yet I felt compelled to assert myself this way because I calculated that the comfort was counterfeit: brief relief now, but down the road, long-lasting feelings of having been deceived followed by disillusionment over God's powers or God's love for her. The patient was deteriorating and it was extremely unlikely that he would improve, let alone live for a long time. (He died about one month later.) My duty was to avoid misguided hope and to facilitate appropriate hope. That kind of hope is about clients feeling they have accomplished cherished goals, or feeling assured that their legacy will be passed on through their loved ones. Their hope might be, if that is what they themselves believe, that they will continue on in an afterlife or even that a miracle might happen.

This next story is about a power reversal, but in this instance it has nothing to do with my voluntarily leveling the playing field or with anyone trying to usurp my role: I had pulled into a cemetery parking lot in Woodbridge on a steamy midsummer's day, being sure to park in a space which granted the sanctuary of shade. There I had counted on placidly awaiting the arrival of the hearse and the mourners. As a car pulled in next to mine, the occupants couldn't roll down their windows fast enough to excitedly unveil the news that I had a flat tire. Sure enough I did, with a big fat nail unforgivingly entrenched there. So much for my meditative reprieve in the shade. But no matter, I figured I could still get in place behind the hearse and make it to the nearby gravesite. As my car uncertainly but obediently limped along, I'm sure in the other cars the topic "The rabbi has a flat!" provided a welcome relief from what lay ahead. I meanwhile was thinking about the grave topic of the three A's and that at least I was in one of the safest if unlikeliest places imaginable to wait for them. I was hoping they would not think it was my idea of a prank: "Hey, I'm at the cemetery and I have a flat!" "Yeah, right-o, we don't have time for your kind."

But right after the burial, two nephews of the deceased rushed over with me the few yards to my car and with the burial mound in full view said they would change the tire. In three minutes "flat" they took off the offending tire and put on the spare, thus sparing me a long and lonely second opportunity to meditate as I awaited the AAA. Members of the family, with the heretofore aloof funeral director trotting close behind, clustered round to say how it was such a shame that this happened. They seemed unaware of the incongruity of how trivial this was compared to the rite of passage they had just gone through, to wit, the sacred conveyance of their loved one to her final destination. With the family helping me as well as my helping them, perhaps it was of some comfort to all present that clergy and mourners alike share the same road, with plenty of detours and potholes before we all have to pull over for good at the very end.

As you will see in Chapter 4, one of those potholes is dementia, which presents a challenge much more complicated than assuring the patient that I am not there to take control. This is because you cannot play by the rules of this world anymore when patients can no longer make sense of them. You can only play by the rules that operate in that patient's reality, which sometimes only they themselves understand.

Chapter 4

"SHE THOUGHT SHE WAS A HIGH SCHOOL STUDENT."
Dwelling Full-Time Within a Memory

When I visit dementia patients, it is like driving in reverse. As dementia becomes more serious, the patient's sense of the present can retreat further and further back in time. As the most recent memories vanish in this trip backwards, the next most recent ones move up in the brain to become the "new" present and so on. I have often had the experience of visiting a patient several times, each time asking her how old she was and getting a successively lower age for an answer. I am always taken aback when someone, who looks like she was born when my parents were, blithely tells me she is fifty years old. These patients are emotionally like the protagonist in the film, "The Curious Case of Benjamin Button," who literally is born an old man and becomes younger and younger year after year until he turns into a baby. That is why an eighty-five-year-old with dementia could tell me he wanted to visit his parents because he was terrifically worried about them. After all, his father was in the hospital, and he had to make sure someone was taking care of his mother. As caregivers of loved ones in this state know, the worst thing to do is to try and set them straight with the "facts" and tell them that their parents would have had to be 120 years old if they were still alive. To refrain from doing so makes sense if you think about it: suppose you were eighty-five years old but you believed you were your sixty-year-old self, and someone right now were to tell you that you are not sixty and that your parents are long gone, your spouse died two years ago, and your grandchildren are all grown up with children of their own. Wouldn't you be terrified and wonder what mad scientist had spirited you into the future?

Better to think of visiting a dementia patient like going on an amusement park ride—full of lurches and surprise turns backward and forward, with hints of leaps of the spirit. I strive to enter their retro-world and see where they take me. Even patients with a miserly output of words can redirect me to a different place. Martha, located in one of the swankier senior centers in New Jersey, resting comfortably in her cozy carpeted room and smelling freshly bathed, for the most part seemed indifferent to one particular visit. During past visits she spoke longingly about her family and eagerly asked me to come again. But whether from her mood that day or from further deterioration, she lay in her bed, awake but not even directing her gaze at me. I felt mournful about her finding communication in this world to be more and more foreign and irrelevant. She did not react to my many avenues of attempted contact, including singing, gently touching her arm, and chatting about her family photos that liberally peopled her shelves. Sometimes all a patient wants is for me to literally just sit as silently as the photographs and not knock myself out to communicate. The presence of another human being can be sufficient itself. But I was unsure if Martha wanted even that, perhaps because I was fatigued by the monotony of seeing so many nonverbal patients that day. So I resignedly got up to leave and as I did so, I heard the first (and only) words from her mouth during that visit: "Too soon."

Aha, I thought, *she wants a 'spiritual presence' after all.* (That's more hospice lingo for you.) Back down I sat. As I took in the stillness, it put me in touch with some feelings of my own I had been stuffing away under the cover of boredom. My tears fought for their release. It was almost as if Martha had sensed (or had she in fact known?) that despite my resistance to slowing down, I needed that quiet time to release some emotions that I had been ignoring. What was bothering me just then? As I just described, there are days on the job when I do nothing but check in on patients who do not speak or are asleep, which we have to do to make sure they are not in pain. Not only that, many of those patients do not try to communicate with me even through eye contact or a nod or a smile, no matter what overtures I initially make. It is impossible to tell if my presence provides any comfort in those cases. It may even be confusing or irritating or frightening.

I have talked with other hospice chaplains about this issue, and one even sighed and said, "Sometimes our job is so mindless." I winced at the truth of that, as you yourself might. You may even be offended if you have or have had a loved one on hospice. You may be fuming, "How could chaplains, of all people, feel this way?" I think it has to do with our wanting to have a meaningful impact on those we serve. We feel so insignificant in the face of death in the first place, so not being able to do anything for our patients, not even communicate with them, only serves to under-score this sense of uselessness. You may recall at the beginning of this book I mentioned that most people wonder how I can do this "depressing" work. My answer is that the issue is not so much the sadness, but the frequent lack of a way to make my presence make a (known) positive difference. I have heard from colleagues that most hospice chaplains go on to other work after an average of eight years.

I think the infrequency of days where patients and families have a pressing need to see us has something to do with this, though for others it may be the opposite problem of having way too many patients to handle, or simply the immense paperwork, which itself does not seem to serve much purpose. One of my colleagues, for instance, was glad to switch from caring for hospice patients to running discussion groups in a substance abuse rehabilitation center. She did this after eight years of serving hospice, right on schedule. "I can use my skills to foster community and be there for them," she said. "We can have discussions and find situations like theirs in the Bible to identify with."

For me, being a hospice chaplain has been a bit like being a security guard. Most of the time is quiet, but when something significant happens, both guards and chaplains put their skills into play for handling a wide variety of possible scenarios. In contrast, my colleague in the rehab center now uses her skills more constantly and regularly.

My mind drifted back to where I was seated, tearful and glancing at Martha in her bed, her large eyes directed at the ceiling. As I got up to leave, I whispered "thank you" to her for helping me acknowledge my feelings of frustration. Dementia patients can be very sensitive to emotion, so maybe she sensed that I had needed to sit there and sort things out. Martha raised no further verbal or nonverbal objection to ending the visit, so I knew my second attempt to exit stage left was okay by her.

Unlike Martha, another patient there named Patty loved lots of attention when someone chanced her way. I usually found her in the lunchroom area of the nursing home, seated in a corner by a window, oblivious to the other residents a couple of arm's lengths away who might as well have been on a different floor. Dementia patients often are unaware of other people unless they are not only near, but front and center in their vision. The staff had told me that she missed her pet beagle, and so she made do with a pile of stuffed toy cocker spaniels, terriers, and boxers that competed for room on her cramped tray table. The luckier ones got premium placement along her arms. After seeing if she would like me to visit (in later days she did not grant me the privilege), I often picked up the dogs one by one and showed them to her. One time I made barking sounds and petted the dogs that were in her arms. Patty smiled at this, and seemed to enjoy the sensation of touch that she was indirectly getting via the light pressure I was putting on the dogs. I then lined up the remaining dogs on the tray table to "wait in turn" to see their master. This may seem childish, but at that moment, that is how Patty and I connected with each other.

In my chaplain intern days, a patient named Millie drove home the quintessential importance of connectedness. She was not on hospice; simply a resident going along her daily emotional travails in a nursing home. I have a record of our interaction and an analysis of it, because as interns, we each had to transcribe some of our interactions word for word as accurately as we could remember as well as our concurrent feelings. We called these transcriptions "verbatims." I had written this particular conversation down because I wanted to demonstrate to our instructor how I coped with and handled Millie's anger.

The instructor was part of a chaplain training program called "Clinical Pastoral Education," which combines classroom seminars with actual face time with patients. Completely trained professional chaplains attend this program for one full year. Hearing strong negative emotions, particularly those directed right at us, is one of our occupational hazards, so the instructor often challenged us to improve our handling of those emotions. Millie, a stout woman in her middle seventies, was infuriated about having to be "in this goddamn wheelchair!" which she felt was a far less desirable option than "being in heaven with Allen [her husband]." She was also angry at being in the nursing home. She felt imprisoned there. (It is not for nothing that the commons area where the residents can socialize or attend activities is called a "day room." The place where prison inmates can similarly be together when not in their cells is called a day room as well! I wonder which usage came first.) As I did nothing to stifle her anger, delegitimize it, or avoid it, she vented some more and the dialogue soon turned the corner:

Chaplain Karen: You say it's all over, it's the end?

Millie: Yes!! I want to be in heaven with Allen! I hate this goddamn wheelchair! I want to be dead!

Chaplain: You are furious.

Millie: [more calmly] You're bringing me down; I need to be cheered up. (This pricks my wonder and curiosity.)

Chaplain: Oh, okay. What would cheer you up now?

Millie: [confused or puzzled] Who are you? Who am I talking to?

Chaplain: I'm a Jewish chaplain.

Millie: Oh, you're so kind to talk to me. [We talk a little bit about Jewish prayers, as I knew she was Jewish and liked to pray. After I sing a Jewish song to her, she laughs and says:]

Millie: I have a sister here. [I'm confused.]

Chaplain: You do?

Millie: You!

Chaplain: Me! Wow! I'm moved. [I marvel at her affection displacing the anger.]

Then, as part of my analysis, I noted that "The staff told me that she forgets visits. She doesn't even remember her brother's almost daily visits, and is not even sure if he's alive." To my surprise, even though I only visited her about once a week at most, she remembered my own relatively infrequent visits more than her brother's. Apparently he was just going through the motions of doing his duty to see her. The point is, she and I connected on some deeper level and she remembered that. I was emotionally more a member of her family (a sister, no less) than her actual brother.

As with my double take when Millie called me her sister, sometimes it takes a while for me to catch on to the private meanings of a dementia patient's world. For example, during a visit with Margarita who was in bed continuously fingering her blanket, it seemed she was not responding to me at all. I had known from prior visits and from her daughter and son-in-law that she liked religious songs, so I kept singing to see if it was just a question of giving her some time to catch on to what I was doing. I did my best to sing in Spanish. Not only did she finally say *"canción"* ("song") among a jumble of other words, she blew a tiny puff of hot air onto my outstretched hand and smiled, as if amused at her unconventional yet somehow intimate way of interacting with me. If I had too hastily dismissed her as "unresponsive," I would have missed out in entering and exploring her secret terrain.

Dementia patients are challenges on every level. Seemingly more than all the rest, they can severely test my comfort zone in hospice work in terms of the level of uncertainty I have to face. This uncertainty ranges from not knowing which people will still be alive on the next day of work, to not knowing what I will find behind the door of that brand-new client, to not knowing when changes other than death may happen, let alone what kind. One of the more perplexing changes has to do with patients who repeatedly go back and forth from deterioration to improvement. I remember the case of Donna, whose plummet downhill fooled the hospice team into telling far-flung family members they better board those planes immediately if they wanted to say their final goodbyes.

I came into Donna's nursing home room after talking with her daughter Elisa on the phone who had just flown in from California. She herself had severe arthritis, compounded with worries about her children's care while she was away, making the flight a major expedition. Elisa, dressed in an ill-fitting pantsuit, was seated on a cushioned chair near the bed reading. Her mother appeared to be sleeping. As Elisa and I talked, I wondered why she did not cast any looks toward Donna or stroke her arm, much less try to talk with her. I myself had spoken with Donna on many occasions, or I should say, listened and tried to make sense of what she was sharing. I knew, of course, that the patient had changed. Her skin looked worn out, like crumpled yellowing paper. And unusual for her, she had been in bed all day long. Still, it seemed odd that Elisa was talking with me as if her mother were not there. Unfortunately the situation grew worse than mother and daughter not communicating. Later in our visit Elisa tried to rouse her mother, saying, "This is Elisa, your daughter." Donna not only did not recognize her, but she aggressively moved her arms around and hollered, "You are *not* my daughter." Ouch. And this dialogue was repeated as Elisa kept trying in vain to reach her mother's mind, after having flown six hours to say a goodbye that could not be received.

About one week later, Donna's daughter was back in California minus any funeral, and I saw Donna calmly and contentedly sitting up in a shared living area, a partially eaten snack on her tray, leisurely turning the pages of a newspaper and repeating out loud to me the gist of some of the headlines much as anyone might over the remnants of Sunday breakfast. The next time I visited her she was the most lucid I had ever seen her, momentarily freed from her dementia prison. She sagely told me about the importance she attached to Judaism and of its function in the world. How unfair it felt that it was I and not her daughter that received Donna's brief zigzag back to connecting with others. From a woman who had not known her own daughter, howled at her, and practically attacked her, I was now getting religious commentary from a woman who understood I was a rabbi. A couple of months later, Donna not only continued to improve, but she "graduated" from hospice back to normal long-term care. Not only that, she had graduated at least one time before, a real pro at "fooling" the entire team of us clinicians yet again. Tragically she had descended into derangement and possible rapid death just in time for Elisa's emotionally, painfully, and financially costly visit, only to rally just days after her daughter had gone home, mission unaccomplished.

Home health aides, the ones on the front lines who do essential basic care like bathing and shaving and feeding, have plenty of stories to tell about their dementia patients. Sometimes they live with their patients around the clock, or at least are with them from two to several hours at a time. Part of how I help out is to listen to these aides and let them vent about their hard work and personal struggles. Many of them have had their own hard lives, leaving dangerous countries and loved ones they rarely or never will see again. They are grateful for any work they can land here. I have met aides from Sierra Leone, Haiti, Russia, various Spanish-speaking nations, and people of color from the United States. Caucasian Americans are so rare they are a novelty.

One day I was visiting a dementia patient in her private home who I learned was becoming more combative than before. When the poor aide tried to touch her to wipe her mouth clean after lunch and brush her teeth, the patient sometimes tried to hit or bite her. After talking about this difficult patient, the aide Carla gave me a rundown of what some other dementia patients in her care had done, including kicking and slapping her. But after she got the distressing examples out of the way, she started to tell more entertaining, pleasant, and even uplifting accounts all topped off with philosophical commentary about their behavior such as, "She used to know who I was, but she still knows I am her friend. God is with her no matter what." I chimed in with one anecdote of my own: "I once visited a woman in a facility named Nancy. Mentally she was back in her school days. But what was so extraordinary to me is that beyond thinking she was a student, she thought the nursing home was a high school, the brightly lit nursing station the principal's office, the dining hall the cafeteria, and that I and other staff were the teachers. The other residents, of course, were her classmates." Carla vehemently nodded her head and made a knowing "uh huh" at that. We agreed that given her dementia, Nancy was better off living in her youthful reconstructed world peopled with her peers and teachers than in a nursing home with no history of rambunctious parties, memorable teachers, and the promise of upcoming family and career goals.

There is no denying that advanced dementia is unspeakably sad, and that a nursing home setting only serves to mercilessly brand that fact into the visitor's unwilling brain. But what is remarkable is that despite all the barriers, sometimes we can reach across the patients' missing synapses and clogged neurons to meaningfully communicate with them, as long as it is on their terms and not ours.

Chapter 5

"What's Next?"
Mutual Musings on the Afterlife

One day I went to see an Orthodox Jewish lady named Miriam, who at this stage in her life felt she could accept a visit from a religious outlier like a female rabbi. (Orthodox Jews do not believe women should be ordained.) Seated in a heavy chair by her bed with a view of the Hudson River from her window, she set aside a magazine to talk with me. Most of her kosher lunch was on the tray attached to the front of her chair. The food had grown cold and odorless and lay mostly uneaten even though it was well past lunchtime. Because I was a rabbi, I suppose, she dispensed with all the small talk one normally feels obligated to preface deeper matters with, especially the first time one meets anyone new. She joined her hands together, interlocking her fingers, and affirmed that she was completely sure that after death she would be in existence somewhere somehow. She was seemingly looking forward to it, and very curious, as one might be about what might be in store for one after some other major change such as a graduation or marriage. She wondered aloud, "What's next?" I half-jokingly replied, "Although our religion says there is an afterlife, it is a little skimpy on the details." Miriam gave me a stern look but then could not resist a smile. I was in awe of her certainty, and on my way back home, the colors of the traffic lights had never looked so vivid to me before, nor the hushed sound of the rain gaining ground over the dry spots on the pavement. The mystery of death is somehow tied to the mystery of all forms of existence, of chaos and order, of energy and matter, of objects and living things, of sweet and sour, of elation and dejection, of stillness and motion.

I also experienced a similar intensification of life when I had a scare about my father one day in 2011. He was ninety then and I got a phone call from my brother that Dad suddenly had to go to the hospital. I had to wait until the next morning to learn that he was fine and was sent home. But the evening before, as I gazed at the plants and fat pens and snack containers parading down one side of the kitchen table, each object looked more intensely present, as if the thought of death was a foil for material things to more insistently signal to me their existence. Perhaps there is a relationship between life and death, not a negation of one by the other. Could it be that both are parts of something even bigger? Do they fit together like two sides of a coin? If so, then we will not end up like a light bulb gone bad. To put it another way, we will not simply cease existing but continue in some fashion beyond our comprehension.

What I know for sure is that we will go to any lengths to deny that death finishes the job. Sometimes on the way to a funeral

I will be lazy about dealing with directions and just ride along in the hearse with the director. Directors tell me plenty of stories about strange behaviors and incidents at funerals. Like me, they also get their share of bemused reactions upon answering the question, "And what do you do for a living?" One director told me during our ride that the most frequent second question he gets after answering that first one is, "Once in the casket and in the ground, do the bodies move around?" Perhaps people ask this not just to back off from death's finality, but to express how inconceivable it is, or at least to put off giving the Angel of Death the last word.

At least metaphorically, people like to speak of the dead as carrying on the same relationships in the next world as they did in this one. One time I officiated at an unveiling with rather unusual circumstances. (An "unveiling" is a Jewish ceremony performed at the graveside approximately one year after the death to mark the closure of the most intense stages of grief.) Sheldon, who had gotten my name from the funeral home's clergy referral list, had lost both his father and his brother within about six months of each other. On top of that, Sheldon told me on the morning of the unveiling itself that his uncle had died a few days earlier, and that he and his family would be attending the funeral that very same day in the afternoon. Some of the family had come from a thousand miles away, and so we indulged in some naughty "two-for-one" jokes about fate having saved them the fare of a second plane trip. Sheldon gestured to his brother's and father's graves, and pointed out that his mother's grave was in between her spouse's and her son's. Sheldon said, "Good thing Mom's grave lies there between 'em. My father and brother never quite got along, and she did what she could to keep the peace. And so there she is where she'll keep the peace between 'em still."

As I am writing, an encounter crosses my mind that inexplicably calmed my own fears that there might be no afterlife after all; that it was just wishful thinking. I had been a graduate student at the University of Texas at Austin and was flying home during a holiday break. Being a dyed-in-the-wool academic, I got into a philosophical discussion with an elderly gent across the aisle about the meaning of life and other weighty matters. At some point I must have expressed my fears about plane crashes or death, because he said, "No matter what, even if we crash, we will be all right in some cosmic sense." Somehow I felt calm and secure after he said that. Perhaps his being older gave me confidence that I would find the inner peace he had managed to acquire. Perhaps his pervasive calm, in stark contrast to my anxious and unpredictable parents, gave me an inkling of what it was like to be taken by the hand even at the edges of the valley of death, where I was to fear no evil.

At the University of Texas itself, there was a second wise soul about the same age who fascinated my friends and me. He was an intellectual who felt his mission was to get into discussions with students to challenge their assumptions. One could often find him in the Texas Union, a building filled with eateries and other places for students to hang out. He was definitely nonthreatening except to those who wanted to remain ensconced in their narrow comfort zones. He was kindly, spiritual, sagacious, and of course bearded. He often stationed himself at a table in The Cactus Cafe to catch the eye of someone to commune with. When we joined him his mantra was, "Everything about each moment is so rich and so astonishing." Although he offered no proof of an afterlife, his concentrated focus on the present shunted my concerns away from the afterlife and redirected them to the everlastingness of now. William Blake had his own version of this wisdom: "To see a world in a grain of sand, /And a heaven in a wild flower, /Hold infinity in the palm of your hand, /And eternity in an hour."

Nevertheless, as attractive as the present is, we are always game for any arguments in favor of the more sought after prize, especially when we are attending a funeral: life beyond the grave. Just as a magnifying glass intensifies the sun's heat on any object beneath it, a funeral forces us into a highly concentrated examination of our mortality and its possible sequel. As we hear eulogies, we hope they will reinforce our belief that there is a sequel to contemplate in the first place.

In 2011, when heaps and heaps of snow were dumped on the ground in the Northeast, I was asked to do a funeral for a sixty-one-year-old man who died of a heart attack while shoveling snow the day before. One of the speakers got up to tell the following Jewish parable: "There were twins in the womb, and one was an optimist and one was a pessimist. The optimist said, 'You know, when we get out, we're gonna have a new and happy life.' But the pessimist said, 'Naah, who are you kiddin'? This is it. We die when we leave here.' The optimist was born first, very happy indeed, but he screamed when he got slapped by the doctor.

The pessimist could hear the scream, and so he says, 'See that? Wasn't I right? He was killed.'" The speaker then said he was not sure how this folktale connected with the occasion. I think it was his wish to be more certain that going from shoveling of snow to being shoveled under dirt was not going to be the end of his loved one's story.

After working for hospice almost seven years, I have heard many patients express their beliefs of what may happen in the afterlife. Usually I hear very traditional ones, such as ending up in heaven or hell. But once in a while I will hear something out of the ordinary that reshapes my own beliefs. Eileen, a ninety-five-year-old elder sister of the deceased, was mulling over this subject with me and said, taking my hand, "I think what happens is different for everybody. We're all different." Then I realized something I never thought through before: instead of thinking there are only two overall choices, such as heaven versus hell, or existence versus oblivion, maybe we have a multitude of available destinations or even designer passageways for each person. Maybe some of us will end up with predeceased family members. Maybe some of us will merge with the energy of the cosmos—a handy Plan B for those who do not yearn to be reunited with their dysfunctional parents. And maybe some of us will resurface in some regrouping of molecules into a new consciousness, or be reformulated whole in another dimension or universe.

In a eulogy I gave at another funeral about the deceased's wonderful marriage, I described a hoped-for afterlife for the couple in this way: "Zelda and Joseph are now both together in a different place. Perhaps this place is a fifth dimension, or another world, or as the tradition puts it, the world to come. However it is characterized, it is a place constructed out of the love that flowed between them. May we all internalize a loving spirit as we continue to walk this Earth, spanning a bridge between this world and the next."

I got the idea for a eulogy like that in the first place because in 2006 I myself had a close brush with death, which made me feel like what I was brushing up against was another dimension. As I was heading home from Princeton, New Jersey to Kearny, I collided with a car ahead of me on Route One North. A thin lone flame appeared under the hood of my Toyota Camry as the hood burst open upon contact, but I knew from my half hour's worth of disaster training that I had to flee from the car without even pausing to pick up my belongings. It took less than a minute for the fire to spread all over the vehicle. As I stood shivering on a prematurely cold day on the side of the road after calling 911, I had the sensation that something from "the world to come" (as Jews refer to the afterlife) was seeping out into this life, and that I was fleeing from that as well. It felt alien, and I knew that I did not want to have anything to do with it at that point in my life, so I did not linger to peer over the edge so to speak. That experience has influenced me to believe that death is an interface between two ways of being, one in our current consciousness and one in some other consciousness.

This sensation of a thin barrier between life and death dates all the way back to my earliest memory of a close brush with death when I was about eleven years old. Several workmen had come to our home to remove worn-out wall-to-wall carpets and install spanking new ones. I remember my brother and I having to sleep in the living room overnight while all the furniture was in disarray. The workers had propped a round marble table top against a chair quite near the spot on the floor I had unwittingly selected to sleep. The top was precariously resting against the chair, and boom! As my brother later put it, "a very local gust of wind blew your hair around as it fell down a couple of inches or so from your head."

That wake-up call jolted me into considering my mortality. The next morning I went to my day calendar, the kind with those tear off sheets where the digits of the date itself gobble up most of the sheet in thickest black, and where the name of the month meekly sits towards the bottom. Sitting at my white vanity desk and looking at our lilac trees in the back yard through my bedroom window, I crammed a few lines on the back of that day's sheet about my first brush with death. Strangely enough, I was not frightened. I was caught up in the mystery of how close at hand death could be. It was only years and years later that I released my arrested fear from its deep freeze. I still puzzle over why I was not frightened at the time.

It is curious that Jewish mystics dwell on the idea of a thin boundary between life and death. They say these two states are more commingled and more alike than we think, and that both are part of something bigger. Jewish mystics also believe that when we die, we go back in reverse through the same steps that brought us into being: They believe that as we become alive, we move from a very abstract spiritual essence of the divine to levels that are more and more physical until we become material beings. Then as we die, we climb back through progressively more and more spiritual layers of the divine until reaching pure energy. This top level, they say, is an outpouring of infinite compassion. And so to me, all of this convoluted abstraction amounts to the belief that when we die, we complete our round trip back home to God.

This calm reaction to being in hailing distance of death continued when I was a student at Oberlin College in the seventies. I was very trusting in whatever fate had in store even during a medical emergency that could have sent me on a very early return trip to my spiritual home. I was in my sophomore year when one day I felt severe pain in my abdomen. In no time I found myself on an ambulance to Allen Memorial Hospital. (Despite the nonstop pain, I distracted myself by speaking with the Hispanic personnel in Spanish! That was the first time my minor in Spanish became very handy. Much later, I would speak Spanish to some of my Latino patients and translate for nurses and social workers.)

The diagnosis was a large ovarian cyst which required immediate surgery. My parents drove in from Erie, Pennsylvania and my brother flew in from New York City for the occasion. At the time, the family scrambling to see me did not sound the alarm in my mind of how serious the surgery must have been for them to drop everything and be at my bedside. In fact, I felt very calm being surrounded by family and friends. Even my Spanish language professor Dr. Harriet Turner stopped by, baffled by my buoyant pain-killer-induced mood as I laughingly recounted practicing Spanish in the ambulance.

As I awaited the surgery, I remember flash-forwarding to a possible scenario of being "sent off" by my visitors if the surgery proved fatal. I think the lesson here is that before our actual time comes, we will not know whether we will be afraid or calm or angry or indifferent. On top of that, I do not think we will be able to relate to the frame of mind we will be in until it happens. To think we can understand this ahead of time would be like asking a child to relate to the mind of an adolescent, or pressing an adolescent to imagine how middle-aged adults view the world.

After finishing up my undergraduate studies at Oberlin College and getting a Ph.D. in Linguistics at the University of Texas at Austin, I became an assistant professor of Spanish at Denison University in 1985. Before that point, nothing particularly challenged my belief in the afterlife. In fact as I said, that mysterious gentleman in the airplane, like an angel in disguise, quieted my fears.

But one day while I was having an early lunch in the Denison cafeteria on January 28th to make sure I would watch the Challenger mission, I of course saw the explosion and then the errant path of the rocket. My first thought was that a tremendous number of high school students were viewing it too, because the high school teacher Sharon Christa McAuliffe was on board. Worst of all, her own students must have been watching. After the horror of all that subsided enough for me to think further, I asked myself how the spirits of the astronauts could have endured the total annihilation of their bodies. Somehow, in a "normal" death, when a body slowly decomposes, it had seemed to me the soul would "escape" to its destination as soon as the last breath was drawn. That was why the Challenger incident was the first event that threw my beliefs about life after death into so much disarray.

So sometimes I think there may be no consciousness of any kind after death but rather a dissipation of ourselves into the general fabric of the cosmos. Science says that matter and energy may be interchangeable, so maybe death is the wormhole that whizzes us from matter to a more energy-like state. I realize it is cold comfort for us to picture our remains reborn into a context far removed from anything we know, or that our identity as distinct beings just up and disintegrates into a whirligig of energy particles rather than arriving intact on our trip back to God. This is not a satisfying view of the afterlife in any meaningful sense of the word. It is scarcely better than being like a hapless fish dangling on a line that will be yanked into oblivion. So on I go, continuing to vacillate between my fear that there is no afterlife to firmly believing in some new home for my inner core of being.

What I know for sure is that even after all these years of occasionally being with persons within minutes or hours of their deaths, I still feel a sense of mystery in their presence. When their eyes are open or half open, I most definitely do not get the impression that they are staring into nothingness. Often they look like they are peering into and preparing for some other kind of reality beyond our ken. I sense the sacredness of transition, as powerful as when I have witnessed persons in other transitions such as newborns, newlyweds, recent converts, and people making major decisions. Could it be that death has something in common with these other transitions? Could it be that as hard as it is to leave the womb behind, or go from being a student to the responsibilities of being a worker, we "outgrow" the comfort zone of life itself and must allow ourselves to dwell in the wider expanse we label "death" for want of a better word? Perhaps those of us left behind really will be joining our missed loved ones in this more flexible arena. In the meantime, the next emotional and spiritual stage of life commences for the survivors, an apt name indeed for grievers.

Chapter 6

"I Call My Own Number Just to Hear My Husband's Voice Again."
Mourners' Trips to the Past

A far more certain "What's next?" after death at least for the survivors is bereavement counseling, a.k.a. "aftercare" in the funeral home industry. The social worker or chaplain on the hospice team provides this to the survivors for about a whole year after the person passes. As I might say with the leavening of a little humor to family at this time, "It's not like we drop you like a hot potato; we are available to call or visit." I then give the details of our programs that help grievers. But nothing in life, not even grieving, can be boxed into a certain time period. You cannot even say, "Well now that your loved one is gone, your grieving will kick into gear." The real deal is that except in the most sudden kinds of death, the grieving gets rolling in advance as you anticipate a death looming on the horizon and you start to take in what that might be like.

Harvey, a spouse of one of my patients, had been married for decades to Lucy. He kept visiting her in the nursing home even after she no longer recognized him. I first met Harvey when I saw him pushing her in her wheelchair in the refreshing breezes scented with evergreen just outside the front entrance. The only change that got him to cut the visits to her way down was when Lucy's anxiety ratcheted way up whenever he appeared. She saw him as a disturbing and unpredictable intrusion into her daily routine. For instance, she got irritable and would not eat when he tried to feed her, while she ate on cue when the health aide fed her. What a blow to find that your spouse is more comfortable and connected with a stranger than yourself! Harvey knew that emotionally and spiritually she was gone from him. After that, he was very receptive to my visiting him at his own home, where he could access a laptop for us to study Scripture.

One way he coped with his wife no longer relating to him as her husband was for him to plunge into religious study. He was a very devout Christian but found my Jewish orientation intellectually stimulating and not off-putting at all. Somehow on a previous visit to his home, we had gotten around to the subject of the Jewish holiday of Purim and to the story about it in the Book of Esther. After I had outlined the highlights of this story, which include the heroes Mordecai and Esther and the villain Haman, he wanted to hear me read it to him the next time I came over. When I did come by that next time, he said, "Well, I very much would like you to read from the Book of Sarah like we talked about." The Book of Sarah? I puzzled over that, thinking that would be great if there were such a thing. Such a book would let Sarah co-star with the more famous Abraham and get another woman in the Bible to figure prominently. Then I figured out he meant the Book of Esther. So I went online and found a pleasantly fluid English translation, and as I read it aloud, I paused a lot so Harvey could bring the Bible alive by linking it to his own life.

The mass destruction in the story, indirectly resulting from Haman's attempt to wipe out the Jews, made Harvey think about the September 11th World Trade Center disaster. His eyes downcast, he spoke of his son-in-law, who had worked as an elevator repairman in the Twin Towers. He had gone into one of the towers to help firefighters get supplies up elevators, and not understanding the nature of the risk, forfeited his life for doing so. We talked about this for such a long time, the laptop reverted to the screensaver, which displayed a commemorative design about the 9/11 disaster. Harvey lamented, "In the Purim story, that guy Mordecai prevented the massacre of the Jews. On 9/11, the massacre was not prevented."

Perhaps you are wondering what I said to that, as it put God in a very bad light: What? Did Harvey mean to say She/He screwed up that second time? I knew that anything but silence and a sympathetic nod, even if I were to present the most watertight elegant and moving defense on the mysterious ways of God, would have insulted his son-in-law's memory and comforted no one but myself. No. The sacredness I seek to preserve and foster in such an encounter is not centered on the Lord "up there," but on Harvey, who felt he could critique God without my censorship.

I was trying to bear witness to the authentic struggles in his heart to make sense of tragedy, and to his complete trust and ease with sharing such forbidden sentiments. He may, now that he brought his negative thought out into the open, in the future feel freer to come up with a revised image of God that "fits the facts."

By the way, I feel the imperative to keep quiet about God and evil all the more so when Holocaust survivors speak their mind. Who am I, who have never experienced even a single one hundredth of their horrors, to have the audacity and hubris to explain away any of their suffering? They are not only mourning the deaths of friends and relatives, but the demise of Jewish Eastern European culture and of a huge percentage of our people. I can only humbly listen and hope they do not think my representing belief in God or even representing a belief in life's meaning is as absurd as excusing God in some way for evil.

Seeing Holocaust survivors has been about the most difficult aspect of my job. Here they are facing death, after having seen so much death, including for some the death of God as they understood the divine. I feel at my most powerless, wondering if it is insulting to overtly offer anything spiritual. Why do they want to see me? To tell God off? To disabuse me of naïve notions? To check out every possible angle for a restoration of meaning or hope? I remember a telephone call from the sister of a recently deceased survivor, where we were discussing the source of evil. When I mentioned the Jewish mystical view that evil comes from imbalances in the universe, for example from power getting out of hand, she scoffed, "That's ridiculous. What insulting nonsense!"

I was not about to argue the point or ask her to explain further, as much as she piqued my curiosity.

A fact about Holocaust survivors that had puzzled me for a very long time was the large number of them who wanted to be cremated. I thought doing that was like giving Hitler yet more posthumous victories, given the fiery disposal the Nazis dictated for the remains of many of the Holocaust victims. Cremation also violates Jewish law, and some rabbis will not even officiate at a funeral involving cremation. Well one day I was reading a news-letter for Jewish chaplains, and the answer popped out at me: they want cremation because they want to feel connected with other Holocaust victims, who perhaps were friends and family, whose fate was likewise ashes to ashes. Maybe in a bizarre way, this amounts to survival guilt in that they do not want the "privilege" of burial.

Getting back to Harvey, after he had dwelt enough on the almost equally dreary topic of 9/11, he moved onto topics that gave him (and me and maybe you now reading this) respite. This is what many patients and family members do, and so it is quite common within the space of one visit to jump from spiritual devastation to their grandson's upcoming birthday party. This time the source of respite was me; that is, Harvey asked what I have been up to these days. I told him I had started writing my very first fiction piece, called "Upward Spiral." He said two very encouraging things. First, "Unlike most people who say they are gonna write, you are really writing." And, "When you finish the book, I want to be the first one to buy it." And so a hospice visit is often like any other slice of life, filled with the bitter and the sweet, the important and the trivial, the humorous and the serious, the incongruous and the ordinary. After that visit, I did not get to see him again, because as his daughter explained, his own health deteriorated to the point that he no longer wanted visits. Eventually, because he had to budget his energy more and more, he could not return my calls at all.

When I describe my work to people I come across, such as unsuspecting fellow bed-and-breakfast guests who my husband and I meet on our travels, they can express discomfort with my dealing with bereavement just as much as with the kind of work I do while the patient is still alive. I am sure some of that discomfort is about their own unease with unfinished grieving or with grief work they anticipate coming up in the future. On the flip side, while this book was in progress, people would tell me I absolutely had to put into the book such-and-such a grief issue they themselves were currently wrestling with.

One day our very exuberant and outspoken financial planner had dropped over to our home and settled on our sofa for a moment of relaxation. The ponderous book *Treatment of Complicated Mourning* by Dr. Therese Rando was hard to miss as it lay on the cloverleaf table we were sitting in front of. "Complicated" means that the extent of grieving is an awfully tough go without the help of a therapist. It also means that the grief is so overwhelming that even after some time has passed, such grievers cannot function at work, or take care of themselves as they normally do, or think about anything else. Or they may engage in substance abuse. Or they may act as if the person who passed did not actually die. In essence, complicated grieving is unhealthy grieving.

By the way, this is not to say that the "run-of-the-mill" griever would not benefit from counseling; grieving has got to be one of the hardest things we mortals are called upon to do in our lifetime. Dr. Rando's tome goes into excruciating detail about the causes of complicated mourning, giving you all you wanted to know about it and then some. These causes run the gamut of a largely toxic relationship with the deceased, to sudden death, to dealing with multiple deaths within a short period, to not wanting to stop grieving for fear of "forgetting" the loved one entirely. I gestured to the book, saying that I had decided to learn more about grief counseling. His response to my endeavor? "I could never get into that. People are complicated enough as it is while the patient is still alive." He perhaps unintentionally made a pun: grieving, even so-called uncomplicated grieving, piles on layers and layers of complexity to one's life, forcing up issues past and present, disrupting family structures, and foisting new roles upon one, and that is just for starters. Added to that is the uneven progress that mourners make: instead of gradually feeling better, there is usually a wrenching back-and-forth between pain over the loss and taking pleasure in sweet memories and current life.

But to tell the truth—and this truth may reassure some of you who are going through this—when I journey long enough with people in bereavement, I often witness spiritual and emotional healing. Ordinarily, the end result of grieving is not death or deterioration but renewed life. Most people go on after sufficient time to life-affirming activities such as making new friends or emotionally reinvesting in a new cause or new project, the knowledge of their loved one's passing now a somewhat softened though perpetual ache.

This is how I described grief in one of my eulogies: "Grieving is a complex process, not a linear progression from more grief to less grief. It's more of a moving forward and a moving back, of taking detours and then suddenly discovering shortcuts, of passing through stretches of tiresome roadways alternated with interludes of peaceful countryside. It is the disorienting journey that will bring you of necessity to a new place, to a renewed place."

Yet, the same as when I visit with families while their loved one is still alive, I never know what I am going to face when I enter a survivor's front door or when they answer the phone. I have run into everything from small talk and affectionate memories, to total relief that the son of a gun is thanks-be-to-heaven finally gone, to a woman whose distress was so severe she wanted me to tell her how to check herself into a mental health clinic on the spot. (The answer to the latter is to have the griever report to the ER and ask for psychiatric assistance.)

Then there was the telephone call I made to a mourner who one time told me about an unquestionably peculiar telephone call of her own. Over the months I had been calling Samantha to see how she was coming along. I had seen her while her husband was still alive, scarcely arousable even for a prayer short enough to be on Twitter. During our last call, she had asked about resources for getting through the prodigious paperwork related to the will or Medicare or some such financial matter. This time she told me something so bizarre about her attempt to contact those resources I just kept talking because my brain said for a while, "This does not compute." Samantha had called some government official or other, and he in turn gave her a number to call to obtain some advice of some sort. "But when I dialed the number, I got a recording that said, 'free sex.' I thought I had dialed the wrong number, and so I called again, and I heard the same thing, 'free sex!'"

After she repeated this again, it finally registered on me and I at first said, "No way!" And then I found it irresistible to joke, "And so did you ask when and where?" (It was a good thing I restrained myself from adding "And for how long?") So we both had some fun with that before I went on to commiserate with her about the disconcerting element of a surprise from a very most unanticipated corner. A government phone number assumed to be associated with Medicare information has got to be the most unlikely conduit to sex talk I have ever heard of, even if an impressive percentage of government officials partake of sexual activity, free and otherwise.

Such stories from mourners are the exception. The usual dialogue I have with them is about their memories of the deceased and how much their loved one meant to them, or how someone else in the picture had meant more. Take for example Kathy, a vibrant eighty-three-year-old who subjected all comers to her home to slushy semi-classical tunes emanating from hidden speakers high and low. I visited her about once a month for almost a whole year after the death. She would sit me down at her kitchen table and feed me some "very healthy granola cookies I made myself." We are not supposed to eat during the job, partly because of the potential to spread disease, but homemade cookies were too hard to pass up.

As she ushered me in, there was always a curious tension between her enthusiastic tone of voice and pleasure in seeing me, and her assertion that she was "in agony" over her husband's death. She had a very involved story to tell, and that is why she had so much to sort out. The man who died, named Roger, was her second husband, who she had wed just six years earlier. Her first husband did not die until after fifty-five years of marriage. All that time, she had known Roger, the one she was eventually going to marry, and had not cared much about the first husband. "Not care much" is an understatement; she said he brought out her meanness and consequently she dished out plenty of it back to him. She found herself in the predicament that she first had to wait for Roger's spouse and then for her own to die to fulfill her heart's desire. Her life had been like having her plate piled up with an uninspiring entrée, and then after managing to get every last mouthful down so as not to offend the host (i.e., society), she only just brushed her tongue against a smidgen of a long-awaited sumptuous dessert before most of it was whisked away.

During the course of the year, she had to sort out her sadness, the loss of her role as wife, her resentment at having to stick it out with her first husband and being cheated of time with Roger, and possibly guilt for not having cared all that much about her first husband. Every time we met, she described Roger in luscious romantic terms: "When we were in the car, I was glad when we stopped at a red light, because that gave us an opportunity for another kiss." Or, "I have left Roger's voice on our answering machine, and I call my own number just to hear his sweet voice again." And, "Every time we ate breakfast, it was like going out on a date." This for sure raised the bar for me on what constitutes romantic behavior. More fundamentally, hearing such tales on the job is a reminder to cherish loved ones while one can, which is one more reason to go on reading a book like this. An added bonus of that particular tale is that I no longer regard red traffic lights in a completely "negative" light.

One of the more curious facts about grieving is that it can kick in well before the patient dies. Not only that, the patients themselves can grieve their own deaths. This may sound strange, but they certainly will not have a chance to do so after the fact. Joking aside, you can certainly feel sad in advance about missing loved ones as well as about the pain they will feel once you are gone. Or a patient may mourn other losses he must endure on the way to the grand finale of death itself. Greta, a patient who was gradually losing more and more of her physical functions due to a neurological disease, told me "for each loss of something I could do and can't do now, like no longer being able to move my arm but just my fingers, I have my own private funeral for it." This struck me as one of the all-out saddest statements I have ever heard from a patient on hospice.

Talking about facing one's death well in advance, I had a ninety-seven-year-old patient who could be witheringly blunt about her concerns about her own death as well as just about everything else. Mrs. Wilson usually turned down my offers to visit, but accepted them just often enough for me to keep trying as I made my rounds in the assisted living section. Her refusals were very abrupt and off-putting, so I had to coax myself to keep giving a knock on her door and not give up. One day she was seated by a small round table sorting through her mail, and deigned to let me in "for a few minutes but that's all." She delegated the task to me of throwing away each rejected piece one by one. (Apparently they and not I were the object of rejection that day.) A wastebasket dutifully stood within tossing range, just waiting to gobble up as many such pieces as it could as if saying "Feed me!" like the ever more demanding plant in *Little Shop of Horrors*.

Mrs. Wilson was mourning her own end, which she could not have been blunter about. She assailed me with question after question concerning her impending nonexistence. It was all I could do to force myself to keep my eyes on her face and not hem and haw. Looking at me as if ready to confirm I would disappoint her by having no answers, she asked, "How do I prepare to die? What do I tell my children?" I talked of reviewing loose ends in relationships and of pondering her legacy, but she rejected those options as readily as the doomed pieces of mail. "I have no loose ends to resolve," she retorted. Given some mutterings over certain family members during former visits, I knew this was hardly the case. But there was no reason to challenge her.

When someone is not ready to examine an element in their lives, then they will ignore any urging to do so. They will not even hear it. Furthermore, I believe that some of the things chaplains and social workers and therapists say to the people they serve are like time capsules. After the visit is long over, the patients may choose to release those words into their consciousness and let themselves ponder their implications. Words that initially were jarring can soothingly cleanse away hurts that had been held in bondage for a good period of time. Before I left, Mrs. Wilson went on to say that my responses to her questions confused her. So Mrs. Wilson was already considering the provocative implications of my answers, while I was left wondering what she had hoped to hear me clarify.

As I said, grief does not occur in a neatly packaged period of time with a clear beginning and a clear end. Grieving does not even necessarily begin at the time a loved one dies. It can start for the family long before "the event," especially if the patient can no longer communicate or does so only in severely limited ways. Grief can extend long afterwards as well, much longer than most of our friends and relatives are willing to believe, who disappear from the scene when mourners need them more than ever. This extended grief can, given the circumstances, still be "within normal limits" as the nurses like to say. Even after several years, a certain event, thought, experience, or smell may suddenly stir up the sense of loss for a little while.

This business of trying to shortcut mourning came up as I was set to officiate at an unveiling, which is a Jewish ritual at the graveside at approximately the first anniversary of the death. Several family members and I were standing around our cars waiting for the rest of the family to arrive before we all proceeded to the graveside. A nephew, perhaps wanting to impress me with his knowledge about unveilings, proudly announced to me, "A rabbi once said, 'Unveilings are not for grieving. They are for celebrating the person's life. The grieving is done at the funeral. The unveiling is a time for happiness.' That is what he told me, anyway." As the nephew said this, not only was I aware that this was wrong or at best just part of the story, but I was concerned about other people listening to us who perhaps did not feel very jolly at all on that occasion. If anything, being at the grave might trigger a surge of sadness or anxiety. So for their sake, as I did not want anyone to suppress their feelings as illegitimate, I simply had to correct him. "Actually, each person mourns differently. The unveiling marks another stage in our mourning journey; it acknowledges that the pain is not as sharp, but there still may be sorrow as well as joyful memories." In a way the nephew may have had the last word, as during the ceremony we all heard Scott Joplin's "The Entertainer" gurgling from an ice cream truck cruising within earshot of the grave. The assemblage was starting to giggle, so I knew I had to comment on it to eventually restore more decorum. "There are signs of the pleasures of life everywhere, even here in the cemetery." They laughed in affirmation, and were then better able to focus on the remaining prayers and reminiscences.

After the ceremony, one of the sons of the deceased offered another sort of reflective comment which he was so taken with that he repeated it to me a few times: "You know, our lives go like those reel-to-reel tape recorders, the kind of recorders we used to have. In the beginning, when all the tape is on one reel, the reel moves nice and slowly, but as you get further along, there is less and less tape and the reel moves very, very fast. Funny how life is like that; every year speeds up more and more." This has to be the most imaginative way I have heard anyone rephrase the tired comment, "The older we get, the faster time goes," which even a centenarian had resignedly said to me. As an aside, I have to say that I have not felt that way about my own life. That may be because I frequently go from one new thing to another, not letting much time pass before I leave one routine for another. (I have a severe case of the "novelty gene.") I think when there is not much change in one's routine, then time seems to pass more quickly. Conversely, when I was in a profound crisis like 9/11, I felt like time did not move at all. I felt that way during the 9/11 emergency for a good two weeks. Mourners too sometimes initially have this sensation of time coming to a halt.

There is another sort of time warping that mourners experience. Very often they feel a pressing need to review and review the months and weeks and days and even hours before their loved one has passed, as if this relatively tiny percentage of his or her life overshadowed much of what went before. One year in May, about five weeks after Passover, I met with Ruth, whose mother had died almost a week earlier. I had attended the *shiva*, which for some Jewish mourners is a period of anywhere from one day to seven when people visit the home of the mourners and in some cases gather to recite prayers with them. After everybody else had gone, taking the soothing warmth of their familiar faces and conversation with them, I had the feeling that Ruth wanted to talk about her mother, even though she had not done so with the other visitors. Sure enough, my bereavement radar was right. As I looked at the homemade religious pictures all around the living room, Ruth started telling me about how her mother was starting to take a turn for the worse around Passover. She had not been eating all that much, especially since for one week much of the fare in her strictly kosher nursing home consisted of the unleavened crackers called matzah. During Passover, observant Jews do not eat bread or other leavened items and so they eat among other things matzah, which is hard and dry, instead of bread which is comparatively filling and soft and moist.

As far-fetched as it may seem, Ruth was about to tell a very funny story about her mom. During this one-week regimen imposed on all residents who were not exempted for health reasons, her mom became a very dissatisfied customer, and therefore was even less inclined to eat. Ruth, knowing full well that her mother's life was drawing to a close, wanted to please her in any way she could. She asked her what she would like most to eat if given the chance: "Bacon and eggs," she said decisively. Taken aback, Ruth repeated, "Bacon and eggs?" From her mom's expression she meant what she said, and there was no getting around the fact that this quintessentially nonkosher dish was among her last wishes. Ruth instantly concluded that the commandment to honor thy mother and father trumped any dietary laws, even on Passover with its more daunting ones to obey, so she decided to try and sneak in the controversial cuisine. All curious as I could be,

I asked, "How did you manage to get past the kosher food police?"

In a satisfied tone she continued, "I went to a diner, ordered the bacon and eggs, and had them packed for takeout. I had a huge purse, one of those squarish looking ones, and so I stuck 'em in there. I then went back into the nursing home and as I got in the elevator I prayed that no one would notice." And in the view of highly observant Jews, here she was, praying to God to allow her to get away with breaking one of God's own laws!

"Incredible," I said. "Seems like someone would have noticed the telltale smell."

"I don't know; somehow I managed to sneak it into her room. She ate some of it and was very, very pleased about it. I felt I had to tell the nurse—the nurses there are not Jewish—just to say that my mother did eat, not to say what she ate; just that she ate, because you know they needed to write down whenever mother ate 'cause she hadn't been eating much. So the nurse did that, just wrote that my mom ate without saying what exactly."

I resisted the temptation to say I was eating up her words and instead reasoned, "I suppose the nurse did that because she was afraid of getting into trouble. What did you do with the rest of the contraband your mom didn't finish?"

With not even a ghost of a smile she intently went on, "A health aide was nice enough to wrap it up good and get it the hell out of there. And what I did was the right thing to do; it was what my mother wanted, and she had not been eating."

I agreed wholeheartedly with her. Besides, even the most observant rabbis adhere to the notion that when commands are in conflict with each other, certain ones regarding the preservation of life, in this case encouraging eating, trump all the rest. Only superficially was Ruth "doing something wrong." On so many other levels she was doing something so very right. On the heels of that anecdote, Ruth rushed on to tell me another of her mother's last wishes, which was, "I will not close my eyes until you and your brother get along with each other again." Happily, over the past few years when her brother and sister had to end an estrangement in order to cooperate sufficiently to ensure proper care for their mother, they gradually became quite loving to each other just in time for her to rejoice in that reunion before she in fact "closed her eyes" for the very last time.

Often mourners talk with me about their loved one's final months, weeks, or even days. The patients themselves talk about the recent past as well, but with a little encouragement they often think back to turning points all throughout their past. It does not take much prompting from me for them to reminisce about their families, their careers, and their special interests and accomplishments. If you think about it, we all like to do this, so why would it be any different when we are near the end? If anything, we have more of our lives to look back on.

Chapter 7

"So How Did the Two of You Meet?"
Reflecting on Life's Key Moments

When I visit patients for the first time, it is like skipping to the very last pages of their autobiographies; it is like involuntarily "cheating" by seeing the end of a story first. The complete history of their life journeys, the setbacks and opportunities, the results of the decisions they have made, the records of their opinions, dreams, and wishes they have had and of the people they have accepted and dismissed, all lie in the preceding pages. In any way I can, I try to work backwards to all the dog-eared and tattered earlier pages to best understand what their past trajectory might have been so I can personalize the visit as much as possible. If no family members are present and the patient cannot speak, objects in the home help tell this story. As I walk in, I might see a plaque conspicuously displayed near the bed proclaiming forty years of dedicated service as an attorney, co-signed by a celebrity. I might encounter wedding portraits with a rustic background, or relaxed poses of family on a cruise who look like they are there as a matter of course, or a photo of the first great-grandchild cradled by some figure who has relegated herself to the background with only her suntanned arms in view. Handmade decorations on the mantelpiece might reveal the patient's interests or talents. I do this type of observation for myself as well as for the client: for him so I can know best how to connect with him, for example by talking about something he likes and is familiar with. For me so I can experience him as a more complete human being, even if all he can do is open his eyes long enough to check out who is talking to him. I often wonder how a patient might have interacted with me if we had known each other in an earlier chapter of his life. Would we have become friends? Would he have enlightened me in some way? Meeting him at the end is humbling in any case, because I might be one of the very last people he will ever see.

When patients are fully capable of communicating, I can get their life stories directly. This is important for them because this is how they can start pondering what their lives have been about and what significance it has had for them and their loved ones. The hospice lingo for this process is "life review." Sometimes I will challenge them to make sense of their lives by asking, "When you look back at your life, what do you see?" More often I take a turning point in someone's life story and go with a gentler approach, for example, by asking a couple how they first met.

I asked an Orthodox Jewish couple that question and got this story from the spouse, Mrs. Goldfarb. Leaning back in her wicker chair in her outdoor patio, she said, "I had met my husband by accident. I was staying in a hotel and heard some commotion nearby. What a racket! I ran outside and saw a car right there caught in the ditch! Well, I invited the driver in to come on in and get all cleaned up; he was all messed up and everything. It was such a shame to see him like that. I felt sorry for him." Because of this kindness, the driver soon wrote out his thanks in a letter to her with his phone number included, and invited her to call him if she wanted to go out. Leaning forward to indicate a shifting emotion she volunteered, "At first I thought he had some nerve doing that, asking me to call him; that wasn't done in my day, as you know." She looked at me intently to make sure I did in fact know. She went on. "I found out later he did that because he would have felt embarrassed if I had said 'no' over the phone."

As Mrs. Goldfarb continued reminiscing about her husband, she added this hair-raising anecdote regarding his life in his native Germany: "My husband had quite a hard life, but was lucky. He escaped the Nazis. What happened is there was this police friend of his that warned him the Nazis were planning to come get him and his family that night. Each family member left the apartment [i.e., permanently] one at a time." I asked her, "Why one at a time?" She answered, "They each left fifteen minutes apart so no one would notice. If they had left all at once, it would have raised the alarm." Perhaps Mrs. Goldfarb, as a result of this reflecting back on Mr. Goldfarb's earlier life, marveled over how such a convoluted chain of unlikely events had ever resulted in their meeting each other.

A widow named Trudy responded to "So how did the two of you meet?" with a description of the most romantic first date you could dream of. She said she first saw her husband when he was playing baseball in their high school field. He came over to her on the stands and "using the oldest line in the world, asked if he had seen me someplace before. I said no, but I sure loved your home run. When I said that, he said, 'Well, I'll go get another for you,' and he went back to the game. That was it for a while, and oh, a long time after that, I was about to go into a movie theater and I saw Ted coming out. So I asked him, 'How'd you like the movie?' and he said, 'I really don't know, I was distracted. I'll just have to go in and see it all over again. See it all over again with you.' And he went in and saw the same movie all over again just to be with me." Trudy had transported herself and me decades and decades back to that first date with Ted as she lay almost immobile on a couch. A nearby blanket with presidential insignia for its subject was ready to provide comfort on a second's notice. In terms of their marriage, she definitely was Ted's First Lady.

Reviewing one's past can reveal what was missing as well as what made one's life worth living. Here is a riddle: Take Saul, a patient in his own home near Hightstown. In his case, what was I able to do for him to fill in what was missing? It was the week of Hanukkah the day I entered his home. He was in a hospital bed smack dab in the middle of the living room, with his wife and son present. I had scarcely introduced myself when the family told me the dreary news that during that very day they had given him morphine for the first time. Then in no time at all, his son skipped any preliminaries and straightaway got to the heart of his father's spiritual pain. "I just want to tell you, something has troubled my father for seventy-two years. My father never had a bar mitzvah." His wife elaborated that because Saul's own father had died right at the time that he was studying for the ceremony, it was canceled and never rescheduled. I mulled this over in my mind, wondering what out-of-whack family dynamic overruled merely postponing the big event. Why didn't they ever reschedule it? Sure enough, later in the conversation, I learned that Saul had always felt ashamed that he had never had a bar mitzvah, especially because his older brother did.

I had an inspiration and out loud I said, "You know what? If you can assemble ten people over here [the prayer quorum needed for the ceremony], I could make him a bar mitzvah at my next visit." Instead of declaring to me that I had to be joking, they talked excitedly to one another picturing the scene of their friends stopping by and Saul saying a prayer. His wife even jumped up out of her chair and got on the phone and started calling the neighbors. In the excitement his son almost forgot to ask Saul, who glowed as he nodded and squeezed out the word yes. Privately I told the family we had better do part of the ceremony right now, as Saul frankly might not be conscious or even alive on another day. And that was what we did. His son trotted upstairs to bring down a prayer shawl Saul's own father had worn, along with a cup of wine. The ceremony consisted of my helping the patient recite the one blessing he remembered, which was a blessing over the wine, and then he just about managed the one ritual sip. I then recited a blessing called the Priestly Benediction. ("May God bless you and keep you. May God's countenance shine upon you. May God's graciousness grant you the gift of peace.") After that I cried out, "Mazel tov! You are now a bar mitzvah!" followed by a traditional song which the family clapped along to and dreamily sang.

I asked if they had a camera handy, and sure enough as good as at any reception they snapped a pile of pictures in a mad rush. His wife then rang up Saul's older brother and put the phone by Saul's ear. I said to Saul, "Wow, here's the receiving line!" Saul proudly told his brother he had his bar mitzvah and the older congratulated the younger. Saul was now spiritually a man. As weakened as he was, he radiated sanctity and supreme joy. Moments later, I was both stupefied and amused by Saul's presence of mind to ask me what my fee would be! I replied that copies of the photographs would be payment enough, which satisfied him. I do have those photos of this Hanukkah miracle, and I treasure the bittersweet pleasure that emanates out of them. One week later Saul died, having fulfilled his lifelong dream.

Somehow as in the case of Saul asking me my fee, I have a way of picking up on humor no matter where I am, even while on the job. Besides the quirky stories you have already encountered in this book, the next chapter is devoted to some interactions which are more decidedly amusing.

Chapter 8

"SAY, ARE YOU A BELLY DANCER?"
Hospice Humor

As unlikely a source for humor as my profession may seem, which you would probably guess is about as "funny as a funeral," I always have an eye out for comical angles. For one thing, as I am out and about visiting patients, I overhear plenty of what other people say on the way to and on the way back from the location I am headed to. One day I was walking down the long halls of an adult community adorned with those safely innocuous resident-generated photographs of swans and sunsets and the like to perk up the colorless walls. This hallway was the corridor that linked the nursing home section to the independent living section within the same building complex. Three ladies who had at least a nodding acquaintance with each other were strolling along the hallway, same as I was. Woman A said, "Huh?" to woman B, who had apparently just said something to her. Woman C then said to both of them, "You know what? The word 'Huh?' should be the password around this place." All laughed, including me.

Woman A, taking in my unexpected relatively youthful presence, then addressed me, "You gotta have humor about these things, about not hearing, otherwise . . . [she made the motion of drawing her finger across her throat]." I gave a knowing laugh, as she had a more appropriate and sympathetic listener than she could have guessed. I had to stifle the impulse to say, "Boy, as a hospice chaplain I know for real you sure got *that* right!"

There certainly was no reason to reveal my true identity, as that would have needlessly drawn their attention to when it would be their own turn for my unenviable services. That is a line practically no one wants to consciously stand in no matter how long and slow it is. I say "practically," because my father used to ask me how old a patient was when I recounted my day's visits to him. If the patient were older than he, he figured that he had some decent amount of time left. If younger, then either he himself had been spared, or it was time to start getting nervous. I think it was the latter, because as he grew older, he stopped asking me about my patients' ages, as the odds in his game of chance were getting slimmer. He also had stopped asking me how many had died in a given week. At any rate, at his ninetieth birthday party in 2011, he confided to me, "I am not afraid of death. Death is peace." That remark had two pluses: it made me feel less afraid of my own demise, and I was glad he himself was not dreading his own.

Besides overheard conversations, sometimes remarks inten-tionally directed at me can be comical. One day I had gone to one of my favorite lunch places, an independent health food store in Princeton called the Whole Earth Center, and for the first time ever in my six years of patronizing that store the cashier asked if I was a senior citizen. I meekly said no and even worse she said, "Are you sure?" as she pointed to a discount for seniors sign. I said "no" again, and she mumbled something about the connection between my gray hairs and wisdom. (At the time this event, I was fifty-five.) A friend of mine teased me for not taking advantage of her wanting to simply give me a discount, but at the moment all I could think to myself was, "Phooey! How dare anyone compare me to the patients I see." Aside from the nuances of the cashier's inner struggle to want to help me out financially versus the risk of implying I am older than I look, this comment becomes funnier given what I heard about my appearance and manner later that same day.

As is often the case when on the job, I dress in a long skirt, a blouse with short or long sleeves, a necklace, and "sensible" shoes. I wear a fanny pack and my ID badge hangs down from a string like a secondary necklace ending in a cloth square with a plastic pocket for the ID itself. If you want to get technical, the string and pocket for the ID is called a "lanyard." I also carry a cloth bag which contains a hand sanitizer, prayer booklet, and some papers about the patients I plan to see. I am also supposed to carry medical items such as latex gloves and antiseptic wipes but I do not bother. I purchased my current bag in Hope, Alaska, which pictures green salmon cavorting against a white background—that alone entertains patients and evokes many expressions of pleasure.

After lunch on the day of the "senior" incident, I had gone to one of the adult communities that contains various kinds of care including a nursing home section and independent living units like the one I just described. As I was breezing along a corridor on the way to an apartment, dressed in a flowing chartreuse skirt and a blouse with splotches of varying blues and white and maroon, the same blouse you can see on the About the Author page in this book, a denizen of the corridor called out, "Say, are you a belly dancer?" That more than made up for the health food whippersnapper's remark about my hypothesized citizenship among the elderly. Even better, later that same day a hospice nurse was still there with one of my patients when I came by to visit. As she wrapped things up like checking his blood pressure, the nurse said, "Oh, there's Karen! She's the one with a sense of humor." Now that is indeed high praise, like telling a coal miner he is good at finding sources of light while on the job or remarking that a funeral director is good at pointing out the bright side.

As in any typical workplace, there is room for humor on the hospice agency bulletin board too. You have your comic strips, your newspaper headlines with unintended puns, and your office party photos that you are glad no one else will ever see. In hospice, the humor about death tends to be gentle. "Humor," keep in mind, is a relative term in my career; do not expect to be rolling in the aisles. I'll settle for a fleeting smile. I recall a drawing that looked like this:

X	X	X
BIRTH	YOU ARE HERE	DEATH

I remarked to a social worker who was happening by when I read this that the cartoonist must have been middle aged. She added, "It sure does make you think about things."

Another way humor can come into play in written form is in our documentation. One of the tasks of the hospice team is for each member to write some information down about each visit and then put it in the digital medical record. This is to make it official that we visited each patient a certain number of times and to show what we accomplished there. So for a nurse, documentation might help her make sure she had given the right dose of medicine to banish pain. She describes the amount given and by whom, and whether there needs to be any changes in the doctor's orders. She can also describe any intractable problems that remain, or new issues, and her plan for what to do next. A social worker normally explains how she helped family members cope better with patient care. Or she may list which community services she directed them to. For me, a clinical note often runs along the lines of how I let the clients vent and the hoped-for outcome for them of calm and comfort from having been heard. Or it might be about my offering prayer and hymns, or for a Catholic patient, about getting a priest to administer the Sacrament of the Sick. Sometimes it is just about making sure the patient is comfortable and letting the nurse know pronto if he is not. Each team member has access to all the other team members' notes on the computer, so we can keep informed and give the very best care. Well, one day I glanced at a social worker's note which said (now here it comes, the miniscule bit of humor!), "The patient was illegible." I am sure she meant "unintelligible."

A much more obscure pleasing resonance to me and to other chaplains who may be reading this book is that in our training we often referred to clients as "living human documents." The gist of the idea is that we "read" what we can about the people we interact with so we can understand who they are and therefore how best to serve them. So if a patient were "illegible," that could mean (if I take this metaphor further) that they were unreadable. Ah well, this association led to a sad thought after all. Sometimes too many pages are torn out of a patient's autobiography to get a sense of them at all. Such is the elusiveness of hospice humor.

To speak of patients as human documents is an apt metaphor, because so much of what I do involves "reading between the lines" to get at what the client hopes I will respond to, but for the sake of saving face does not want to come out and say explicitly. Or as the American psychoanalyst Theodore Reik put it, I have to "listen with a third ear." You may remember the case of the patient named Bob, his wife Jill, and the devout friend Anna who prayed for and preached at length to the couple (see Chapter 3). After Bob's death, Jill said yes to my offer to come over and visit her. As you may recall, we members of the hospice team can make ourselves available to call or visit the bereaved for up to a year, for thirteen months to be exact. Usually, survivors take me up on this offer when they want to vent their feelings or simply want information about what to expect as their grief journey lies ahead. When I went to see Jill, she did not want to discuss either of those things. We sat and drank tea and ate cookies, talking about nothing in particular and having a great time schmoozing. I was happy enough to be invited to high tea and have a respite from intense conversation, but I was puzzled as to why she wanted me to come over. I finally asked her if she had anything particular on her mind, and she said no. She even embarrassed me by asking whether I only could make visits if there was a problem to discuss, but still left me wondering why she wanted me to come. I wondered what I was offering that her friends and family were not. They too had been visiting her regularly.

About a month later, I called to see whether she wanted another visit and promised that I would just be there to enjoy high tea with her again. At the visit, after a brief discussion of a family problem, we once again just enjoyed chatting. Something she said tipped me off that the message I was to read between the lines of this human document was simply, "I am lonely for a person who just wants to enjoy my company." Sometimes I am looking for deep complicated reasons for things, so the joke was on me that she simply wanted companionship. Since she did have other visitors, a footnote to her text was probably, "And since you are a clergywoman, it is like having God drop by for tea and cookies and juicy gossip." As for her devout friend who had also continued to visit, maybe Jill wanted me too so that I could just represent God being in the moment with her without any agenda to persuade or convince her of anything.

Another venue where humor can rear its pretty head is at the interdisciplinary team meetings. These are usually super serious weekly discussions of the patients in which funny remarks and even gallows humor are a welcome comic relief. Every week or two, the whole team sits together along with a doctor and clinical supervisor, to go over the whole list of patients to review what they might need and to give the team a more holistic view of each. We also get up to speed on information such as who is rapidly deteriorating, or who might "graduate," that is, go off hospice if they are continuing to remain stable or even improve. These meetings can overwhelm us since almost always we are hearing about one doomed case after another with all the attendant physical, emotional, and spiritual gory details. So along with the impending death itself, we sometimes have to hear about such things as family members leaving a patient alone all day, presence of guns in the home, intractable pain, and recent or impending deaths of other family members besides the patient. Especially for chaplains and social workers, who do so much listening all day already, we may want to just stop up our ears and indulge in ignorance as bliss. So when something incongruous crops up, we all laugh like crazy; laughter is our sweet escape hatch.

At one such meeting, the nurse was describing a peculiar family. She said each time she visited there, she would bonk into a low lying chandelier on the way in. "The funny part is that instead of raising the goddamn chandelier, the guy's wife wrapped it with bubble paper so that when we visit it won't hurt as much–'As much.' Can you get that?" You probably aren't consumed with fits of giggles, but then again, unless you are a hospice worker, you do not need as much of an excuse to burst into laughter. We will stoop to laughing at just about anything, which means the humor can be quite dark. (You might want to skip the rest of this paragraph and the next two if you are a gentle soul or recently lost a loved one on hospice.) One of the things we mention a lot during the interdisciplinary team meetings is how much weight each patient has lost in the past few weeks or months. This is an important indicator as to whether the patient should continue receiving hospice care, meaning she should if she has not stabilized for the long term or even improved. So once in a while, team members on the heavy side will sigh and wistfully say, "Ah, the hospice diet. I should try that."

Another time I induced the humor myself. At one of the hospices I had worked for, United Hospice of Rockland, the custom was for the chaplain to offer an opening prayer or inspirational reading to set a respectful tone. Since my singing was sought after even by staff, I would offer a religious but not too religious song, such as, "He's Got the Whole World in His Hands." I say "not too religious" as I had to keep in mind the diversity of religions or absence of religion of the team members. Well, one time after several days of record humid ninety-five degree weather, instead of the expected solemn hymn, I rang out with the 1945 Christmas carol "Let it Snow." That evoked a prolonged chorus of laughter.

Then there was the time I unintentionally made a very bad pun, but fortunately just to my husband Steven and not to the grieving family. It was about twelve degrees Fahrenheit with winds gusting to thirty miles an hour and I had to do a graveside funeral. When it is cold outside, a cemetery feels colder than the reported weather conditions because it is a wide open space with plenty of room for wind to cavort in and for chilling thoughts to discomfit us. When I spoke with the deceased's son about his preferences, he readily agreed that because of the extreme cold, the funeral should be mercifully brief. As I prepared the ceremony, I felt torn between sufficiently acknowledging the loss by including all the most essential prayers, and not making the mourners (and me) suffer from the so to speak bone-chilling cold. Now that is a pun too, but what I was thinking of is that as I described this conflict of doing a proper ceremony versus not making people physically miserable, I said to Steve, "I guess I will have to do a bare-bones funeral." As soon as I said it, I realized how awful that sounded, and as I said it did not reach the ears of the people involved. Nevertheless, I could not resist a wicked smile to myself at the thought, nor as you can see including it here.

But please do not be too outraged at these reminiscences of dark if not downright disturbing humor, because sometimes the families themselves indulge in comedy that flirts with sacrilege and they laugh just as loudly. One such family and I were at the graveside. The deceased had moved from one displeasing dwelling to another many times in her life. As they were reminiscing, her sister said, addressing herself to the grave, "Well, Madge, this will be the last apartment you will be moving to. You better be satisfied that it is a good one, because it's gonna be the very last." It's a wonder that she did not praise the long-term cheap rental rates.

A more intricate case involved a patient and wife who had a sense of humor that was so contrarian it fooled the hospice team into thinking the patient had been abusive to the spouse. On the contrary, humor that now and then bordered on sarcasm and irony spiced up their relationship as far as I could judge. Malcolm could dish it out but Becky could sure send it sailing right back. As he spoke to me, Malcolm made many ironical comments about his "ticker" and his impending end, smiling and with eyes flashing as if it were all a ruse. I think he was playfully daring me to feel uncomfortable about referring so casually and indifferently to his prospective cardiac demise. Meanwhile Becky tried to dismiss his hints of being heaven-bound as absurdly premature.

Becky took Malcolm outdoors from time to time in the car to give him a break from just endlessly sitting and sitting in his easy chair. They would see some park or go to a drive-in window to pick up some simple fare. One fine day, the final day it turned out, she took him to a McDonald's. He ordered a burger, and proceeded to eat it in the car on the return trip. They did not both make it back. At least not the whole way back. Mid trip, burger consumed, he leaned sideways and his ticker timed out and ticked its last tick. When I saw Becky several weeks later, as devastated as she was and guilt-ridden for having taken him out of the house and tired him, we both could not help bursting out laughing at what a terrible burger he must have eaten. I simultaneously thought to myself how in my college days those of us who were passionate about health food had given the local Burger Chef the moniker "Burger Death."

Related to humor on the job are discussions that are not funny but are ironic or incongruous enough to be darkly amusing. It was the last day of April and a couple I was visiting for the first time gaily invited me to sit with them on their outdoor deck overlooking their flower-filled garden. The patient and his wife just wanted to be in the moment, so I chit-chatted about the kinds of flowers and trees in the garden and about the history of their dead-end street. They had plenty to say, having lived there for over fifty years and possibly married for even longer, so I did not have to say much to prime the pump for conversation. The patient, who loved gardening, morosely alluded to his no longer being able to tend it.

His wife then pointed to a neighbor's rotting tree, some of its branches jutting into their own property. "I don't like dead things," she asserted. "They should be removed. See that tree? [She gestured to a great big one in the center of their garden.] It's pretty much dead. I'm afraid it will have to go. It will be such a big loss; we've already had to cut off so many of its branches. I hate to see it go; we've had it for such a long time." I thought to myself, how could she say she does not like dead things? Here she is unaware that her talking about death and removal and big losses was foreshadowing another sort of big loss: right next to her was sitting a man who himself was slated, so to speak, to be removed as well.

Sometimes humor arises out of challenged assumptions. One assumption the team makes too hastily is that when we visit patients they will be thinking of profound things like The Meaning of Their Lives, or Last Words They Want to Say, or How to Prepare for Death. The reality is a patient often will want to talk about everyday trivia, treating their last days much like all the preceding ones as if to say, "I'm just as much alive today as I have been any other day." One of my open-ended questions I use to signal that I am there to listen is, "What are you thinking about now?" I asked this of a supremely intelligent man who had been a lawyer. Ralph had imparted many wise lessons to me such as, "If you were to have just the judge decide a case, he often would come up with the same decision as a whole jury." He was bed-bound, and he whispered so softly that his voice was soft even by whispering standards. When I asked what he was thinking about, he often mentioned music because he knew I could sing and he liked me to do so. He was so knowledgeable about music and his memory so perfect that eventually he grew tired of my limited repertoire over my many visits and he asked, "Don't you have anything else you could sing?"

At any rate, it was around the end of March when I asked him again what he was thinking about, and as I leaned in to hear his momentous thought he replied, "Federal taxes." And not only that, he informed me that "estimated taxes help the economy." The incongruity of a dying man talking about the intricacies of our tax code made me think of Benjamin Franklin's assertion that "in this world nothing is certain except death and taxes."

How is it that I have ferreted out quirky stories like these in such an unlikely setting as hospice care? On the most superficial level, I think humor is a way to enjoy life even when we become very conscious that we can no longer take being alive for granted. I have often used humor to give patients and their families momentary relief from all the oppressively serious things on their minds. When I introduce myself, I frequently take advantage of the singsong coupling of my last name with my title, "Chaplain Kaplan," which is good for a laugh, especially if I accompany it with a sly smile. (I once wrote a fictitious verbatim dated April 1, 1998, where the patient quips "And if your last name were Chaplin you'd be Chaplain Chaplin.") Whenever possible, I highlight something patients and family members say, such as an unintentional pun, and make them laugh. Being receptive to spontaneous sources of humor inherent in the very nature of human interaction gives me a break too from the forbidding seriousness of it all.

Still, it seems that I utilize humor to a greater extent than most hospice chaplains; after all, I have a reputation among staff for being funny. What might the deeper reasons for that be? In one respect, I am comfortable with distancing myself enough from a situation to see it from multiple perspectives and thereby not have much of a stake in it one way or the other. Even more basically than that, I take what I just said about distancing myself and I think about how I have done that before. As a child, I was socially on the outside, and that was what I was used to, not that I ever liked it. When the playground lines formed after recess, I was always the last one in line. If there were an odd number of children, then I did not even have a partner in that last spot. When I did, that child did his best to let me know he was beside me only under duress. On the one hand, my isolation made me sad and lonely, but on the other, I could take in details that the people "inside" were too enmeshed in to be aware of. In the end, this ability as an adult to get outside of a situation so I could look at it more objectively endowed me with the means to undo the lack of nurture at home that garbled my social language beyond recognition. This isolation coupled with my misunderstood or even unacknowledged listening disorder pushed me toward introversion.

I think the subversive side of humor has some connection with my distancing tendencies as well. Humor can challenge the status quo. It upends assumptions and therefore can threaten those in charge. When I sang "Let it Snow" during that hot day at the team meeting, my colleagues laughed in merriment, but not our supervisor. She apparently took my act as too cavalier toward her desired atmosphere for the meeting. For good or for ill (that supervisor eventually let me go), my sense of humor has provided another means of keeping my distance from the mainstream, even if that mainstream itself (the hospice agency) is off the mainstream of society in general. As a result, as a jocular hospice chaplain, I have been living on the edge of the edge!

Chapter 9

"YOUR TEARS ARE JEWELS."
Having a Go at Telling My Own Story

Between existence and death, our lives are works in progress, unfolding like the lives of characters in an unfinished novel. While writing this book over a period of two years, I watched my own life moving forward, partially shaped by the writing itself as well as by how clients, colleagues, pre-publication readers, and I converged upon each other's lives. Now that you have learned of so many of my clients' stories, perhaps you may wish to know more of my own life story. To that end, this last chaplain encounter consists of an imaginary scenario where I am the one being "chaplained"—where the time has come for my own final chapter.

I will grant myself a long life in this imaginary meeting and be ninety-one years old. I take this liberty because a mortality survey projected that I would live until around then—I have no argument with that! Given my family medical history, most likely I will have something wrong with my heart in my final days but will be of sound mind. I picture myself living in my own home with my husband, as I do not wish to cede any control over my day even though it means I will have to invest much more effort in maintaining social interaction. The hospice chaplain, highly experienced and board certified—that is, I have met my match—will be visiting me the day after tomorrow. I had said yes to her initial phone call asking if I would like a visit. I said yes because if nothing else, I was curious about meeting a colleague. Curious and hungry for experiences to the last, I want to see what it will be like to be the one listened to in this situation instead of the one listening. I always had wondered about that. Not that I was in any hurry to find out! I wonder what it will be like to answer her questions such as, "When you look back at your life, what do you see?" What will it feel like to have a chaplain say to me, "How lost you must have felt before you found your place in the world!" Or to answer questions like, "What would you say were your most significant struggles, accomplishments, and pleasures? Why did you choose to be a hospice chaplain?" What will I ask that chaplain—she said her name is Darleen—in return?

Chaplain Darleen makes her first visit to me on a mild breezy day in the late spring of 2049. The smaller branches on the dogwood tree out front are flapping around madly while the heftier ones manage to hang on in a more dignified manner. A thunderstorm must be waiting in the wings. I can still walk (or "ambulate" as hospice workers love to say as a linguistic badge of professionalism), and I set out to answer the door, one of my mini-expeditions of the day. Due to shortness of breath, I head back to my easy chair as soon as I can, and invite my guest to have a seat in the chair's twin. I mischievously tell her I want to give her fair warning I had worked as a hospice chaplain myself. She deftly replies, "Then I better not go with those stock responses like, 'What does that feel like for you to be telling me that?'"

I joke back, "Well, why not, and just think what a great verbatim you could get out of this visit!" There I go, funny 'til the end.

She laughs, somewhat self-consciously, and probably is wondering what kind of ride she will be getting.

I remember my own sense of feeling presumptuous when I had to be a chaplain for any kind of clergy. Would a brown belt give lessons to a black belt karate master? However, as any good chaplain does, Darleen uses the fail-safe strategy of remaining quiet to see what I will choose to bring up next. I put off getting to anything too deep by doing what I normally do, which is to inquire all about the other person, resulting in my listening more and talking less. Then I think, *To be honest I tend to do this because so many times people (read: parents) had not patiently listened to me even when I had something pressing to say.* So guarding against the disappointment of potentially not being heard, I just say, "I'd like to hear all about how you got interested in chaplaincy, about your training and all."

She gives me a brief overview and then prompts, "Rabbi Karen, tell me about your chaplain journey too; this is so inspiring to meet someone with your experience. It's so exciting to meet the author of a hospice memoir. And I do wonder, as you say in the book, what it's like for you now to be the one visited and not the visitor."

"You know about the book?" I pause to catch my breath. "I knew the general public were afraid to hear about hospice, but in spite of themselves were curious enough to at least peer over my shoulder and see why we do work like this. Though I think there are plenty of other jobs out there I could never picture my own self doing, like being a proctologist or working in a poultry factory. Yet people do 'em, right?" Darleen grins and says "uh-huh" and once again, can intuit when to stay silent. Thank God she is not distracted and is tuned in to me. "Anyway, I found my place in pastoral care. I found the sacred in the meeting space between me and the patients. They talked with me about what really mattered; there was more room for authenticity. Even right now, we have this great opportunity to talk about special things. I'm not one to do much small talk, though sometimes it is relaxing to do that. Like you, I too always have wondered what it would be like for me to be the one visited by a chaplain, be on the other side of the bed so to speak. In the book, I wrote an imaginary meeting and got my wish in advance. Though it sure is way different now from what I wrote then."

"Different?" she asks as she leans forward, her glowing amber necklace hovering over her lap. "How so?"

I think for a moment and reply, "It was a little scary putting myself in that scenario, picturing myself being near the end. It was damn spooky calculating that it would be 2049 exactly 35 years later from then. Of course I've thought about how long I might live, but I never before thought what actual year might appear on my tombstone. And now here I really am; you would think I'd be more scared. But it's more like, something abstract is going on, almost like—see that round marble table over there? It's still with me; my dad had it until he died. That's the one I wrote about, the would-be murderous table that missed me by inches and I just marvel—I exist and almost stopped existing then—I am so amazed at the idea that we exist at all, that we are now here right at this moment talking, that the world is here. The truth is, maybe I just can't take in what's happening to me. Can't get my arms around it, can't wrap my mind around it. How can it be that all this existing is going to become non-existing? Or that we will exist but in a way unrelated to anything known?" I wonder how she is comparing what I wrote in the book about my imaginary visit with a chaplain with what I am saying now. Somehow I feel reticent about asking her.

Darleen does not let me meander too far from her initial question: "So now tell me, what's it like for you to be visited by the chaplain instead of you being the chaplain and visiting your patients?" She and her swinging necklace settle back in the chair. She waits despite my initial silence.

I listen to the exuberant wind outdoors. It has built up like Ravel's Bolero. Nature frolics along at a mounting pace as I start to ever so gradually coast to a stop. "Well," I tentatively begin, "it's like I don't have to do my leave-taking alone. Like you will walk as far as you can with me, to the very edge, and that you will wave goodbye even after I can no longer reach you in this dimension. We are almost betwixt and between, aren't we?"

Darleen is silent before my directness, perhaps feeling helpless as I so often had, knowing that I could only accompany my patients up to a certain point and they would have to complete the last step beyond where I could go. I resume, "I wrote a lot about being at the edge throughout the book. Now here I am at my own ultimate edge. And I'm stuck in the same vacillations I showed in the book. I went back and forth in it about believing and not believing in an afterlife.

I still alternate between fear and composure about my own end as I go through the real thing. I am entranced by the mystery of it all, and yet sometimes I feel indifferent and sometimes I plain old panic. Ha! How's that for ambivalence?"

Darleen now picks up on my shift from sadness to the faint but telltale trail of anger I am leaving in my comments. "So, tell me about your ambivalence," she says with an ironical smile.

For some reason, maybe so I won't have to think about my own Act 3 Scene 3 for the moment, I think about the ambivalence I developed toward my chaplain career after about five years.

I get up for a moment out of my chair to stretch out my legs and then lower myself back down. "And as wacky as this may sound, Darleen, that's why I finally switched back to a teaching career; I ended up teaching English to immigrants, first at Hudson County Community College in Union City, New Jersey as I had done there fifteen whole years prior. If you'll pardon me for saying so, I became restless with the hospice job because a whole pile of new bureaucratic requirements forced me to visit patients who did not need me there or from what I could tell, did not even want me there. What I mean is some patients consistenly turned their heads or bodies away from me or had otherwise sealed themselves in their own world. That world included an opening, if there was one at all, only to loved ones. They could not literally tell me to stop visiting, so the hospice agency requirement was to keep seeing them. How I hated doing purposeless work. Well, I've griped enough with you. I'm just telling you how hospice had changed in those days. But you know what? It sure was revealing how family and friends had reacted to my latest career zigzag back to teaching."

"How do you mean?" Darleen looked fully absorbed; I hope I was not rubbing any sore spots in her own work experience.

Once again I had to pause to catch my breath, and to husband my energy. "When I switched to teaching, the same guy who commented on my book about complicated grief said, 'Well, at least you won't have to watch anyone drool anymore.' Ha-ha, what an image! I guess he meant there were repulsive or just plain sad elements to the job. And then my brother's reaction was, 'It's healthier that you are doing something else now.' Funny he said that, because the Montanan author Ivan Doig implied the same thing in his novel *Work Song*." I reach over for a copy of it, the old fashioned physical print kind, lying on a round green table with fluted sides right next to my chair. I had been rereading it, which is what I always do with good books. I turn to around page 136 and first explain to Darleen before reading it to her that "it is about a newcomer in town, staying in a boardinghouse, who takes up any job he can to pay the rent. He gets hired to represent a funeral home at wakes. After some time, the boardinghouse matron says that despite the fact that the job brings in the rent, she hints against 'the reasonableness of that as a lasting occupation.' Somewhere soon after that, Doig then says the newcomer leaves that position and takes a job as an assistant librarian. And so I too reached the point I guess where hospice was no longer reasonable to continue as a lasting career."

Darleen reflects on this and replies, "But I think that's more about how society is uncomfortable with death and the people who have jobs connected with it like funeral directors and hospice chaplains. But beyond that, what do you think your own deeper reasons for leaving hospice were?"

I nod. "Hmm, it's kind of ironic that I picked a vocation where I did lots and lots of serious listening. I had to take people very seriously. When I was growing up I was not listened to. I was not taken seriously because my parents were too burdened with their own problems to be emotionally available. Well, maybe my choice of profession was not so ironic. I've heard that people try to heal themselves by doing for others what they themselves didn't get. I had to make my own way, with its benefits and burdens... Oh, I just realized something. You asked me why else I left hospice. I think another way to put it is why I returned to teaching. ("Uh-huh," she says, probably wondering where my medley of ideas is leading.) As much as I was comfortable listening to my clients, sometimes I chafed at having to hold back. I mean, I was always listening and I had to make space, a sacred space surely, to make room for their words. But this meant I rarely got to talk, even more rarely about myself, and of course never talked about my own concerns and opinions. I tell you, sometimes this whole listening business is just way too passive. I think I talked more as a teacher during one class meeting than I did for a whole month of patient visits."

"So you had to withdraw yourself in some ways," Darleen suggests. "And of course I know what you mean. It's the only way to be a good chaplain. And the teaching?"

"Well, there I did plenty of talking, as I said. I could give of myself through explaining the subject matter, through editing the students' work, through all the pleasure of back and forth conversations with individual students. I challenged them, I encouraged them. So you see, I was the one being listened to. Paid attention to. And it didn't hurt to be away from all the sad scenes and having to think about death so much."

I trail off and fall into a reverie. She strokes my arm and repeats my comment about growing up bereft of proper emotional connections. I explain that if I were to tell her all the peculiar things I had gone through, she, like others who have patiently heard me out, would marvel at my survival and at my successes. Things like my mother encouraging emotionally lost people to hang around who as a child I found strange or even threatening. First I told Darleen about black-haired Ron, who always wore black from turtleneck to shoe and who felt depressed and tossed around suicidal thoughts from time to time. Mom kept hoping she would help him, and that his conversion to colorful attire would advertise her success. That never happened as far as I know. The blackness endured.

Then there was a Dr. Ferris, who had sunken cheeks like plenty of my patients, smoked a lot, and had a whiney yet lilting voice. He had a substantial piece of rural property where someone took care of his twenty-odd cats. I saw them once on a trip out there, stiffly prowling about in their cages, perhaps resentful of their lot. I had puzzled over why he had so many, especially since he did not see them very often. As the king of all hoarders, he even bought a defunct library, the Weis Library on Old Sterrettania Road near Axe Murder Hollow Road, in Erie, Pennsylvania, to store all of his detritus in. (Erie legend has it that Weis Library was haunted along with the hollow!) At least he was kindly. I remember one time he placed some Japanese and Chinese jade figurines on the round marble table and told me about them as I stared at them, entranced.

But there were less benign characters than Ferris and definitely far more disturbing ones than Ron among Mom's friends, who I have classed privately to myself as "Mother's Coterie" ever since I can remember. These other members spoke loudly, drank copiously, smoked incessantly, and, worst of all, made mention of sexual subjects. All of them either had mental illnesses or some other marginalizing features. Mom, as queen of these remaindered souls, made our home their social center starting when I was ten, emotionally displacing me to last in line.

But worse than that, I tell Darleen, my parents failed to shield me from the coterie. "Sometimes many of them were visiting all at once, a real witches' Sabbath if you ever heard of one. Even now I tremble to speak of it. To top it all off, there was even a person with a murder record who had lengthy telephone conversations with my mother. I read online that about forty years later she killed again, involved in a bizarre plot where she forced one of her victims to rob a bank by making him wear a bomb collar that would go off if he did not cooperate within a limited period of time. And he had to carry a cane-shaped shotgun. So awful. In the end, the collar actually exploded and killed the guy." As I am telling this to Darleen, I remember this crime grabbed national media attention. Wikipedia reports that the CNN television news show *Anderson Cooper 360* "highlighted the story as one of the FBI's most mysterious cases." What an Addams Family existence I had! But actually such a family as the one in that TV show would have done a better job of taking care of me because of their compassion for each other and their visitors, their relatively safer environment, and their joy at being who they were.

"Because of my childhood setting," I conclude to my chaplain, "I have often said that my epitaph should read, 'Against All Odds.'"

She falls silent with a rapt expression. What is she thinking? The jazzy improvised dance of conversation is such a mysterious process.

She says softly, "Karen, you sure did survive against incredible odds. I can scarcely fathom how you made this amazing achievement of rising above adversity, and not just to get by, but to excel in so many ways; emotional, intellectual, and spiritual. After years of chaos with your Mom's not only odd but downright dangerous coterie, you managed to beat all the odds against achieving high self-esteem—meanwhile contributing to society, being creative, and flourishing alongside your loving husband since 1989. 'Against all odds' sure should be your motto."

I look at her, waiting. I am tempted to just close my eyes, I have dug down so much. Then I meet Darleen's compassionate blinking eyes and see her hands rub her cheeks. I see my own sadness entering her burdened eyes, her face, her fingertips. She then asks in the gentlest voice, "Karen, how *did* you beat such daunting odds as those?"

"I don't fully know. This whole business has puzzled me so much, because of another question: How come some people are *not* resilient enough to recover from the damage? You know, I did come to something of an answer for a memorial service I'll never forget. The man who died was a public figure who himself had suffered multiple kinds of adversity, like poverty, medical problems, and ethnic discrimination. But he flourished and became world renowned. He wrote an autobiography, and he pondered his own resilience just like I'm doing now for myself. [The survivors have requested I do not allude to his or her identity.] Anyway, in my invocation—you can read it for yourself—it's in the file marked 'eulogies' over there in that metal cabinet. Look under 'E.'"

Darleen goes over and gets it and reads aloud a few phrases from the end: This person "seized upon his own internal flame that had been waiting to illuminate his life purpose. Each of us has a flame residing within. It may be sputtering. It may be tamped down by malicious moisture. But with the unfaltering fan of passion, each of our own flames will blaze their way into a most exalted and full and bountiful panorama of light."

"You see," I continue as she looks up from the text, "This sort of says if too much moisture is dumped on the flame that we all have, then we won't make it. And believe me, I've met plenty of people like that, like Mom's emotionally-ill friends for starters. It's the saddest thing for me to come across people who can't surmount their past." I pause, thinking of something I read in a John Cheever's novel, *The Wapshot Scandal*, where he talked about such people: "We are all ransomed to our beginnings, and for some people, the sum might be exorbitant." I then add, "Those people have permanently fallen in a pit and I cannot reach them and pull them out. And sometimes I feel afraid as I think how precariously close I have been many times to tumbling right down into the pit with them permanently and being trapped there. But somehow for some people like me, even a faltering flame can keep on going because of the passion inside there that fans it. Though I guess that still leaves the mystery of where the passion comes from." (I pause to catch my breath.) I ramble on: "It's tempting to say it's from God, but then I don't understand why some people's destiny is to have enough passion to overcome the bad stuff while others are not so lucky."

Darleen ponders this but she sees I am way too tired to continue, and tells me she can come back another time. Then in the ensuing quiet after she closes the front door after herself, I think to myself the factors that allowed me out of the hole—the pit, like Joseph was in—have varied over the different stages of my life. Like when I was a child at home, my family revered fine music and classic literature. I transcended my otherwise cramped emotional space by soaring into uplifting music and losing myself in the emotionally safe world of literature. A cherished memory is of my father frequently playing a recording of an opera and giving me the libretto complete with translation to follow along as I sat in an easy chair with an ottoman. For some reason it sticks in my mind that one of the records was made of red vinyl unlike all the other black ones, which fascinated me to no end. I eventually became familiar with the melodies of over a hundred classical pieces, which has given me the lifelong pleasure of recognizing them when played on the radio or at concerts.

Another pleasant memory I have is of the whole immediate family, the four of us, reading books at the same time in the living room; a rare oasis of mutual quiet enjoyment. My mother was an avid reader of such authors as John Updike, Saul Bellow, and Philip Roth. She not only wrote to some of them, but at least one (Saul Bellow) even replied to her insightful comments. A handwritten letter of his which is in my brother's custody includes the comment that "Rabbis are to God what brokers are to real-estate. I've seldom known them to be very godly." My response to that sentiment is "Ow!"

Perhaps this literary milieu was what led me around age twelve to plunge into creative writing, finding haven in the arts on the other side of the pen so to speak. Then starting in high school I constructed my own inner orderly world out of academic pursuits. I wrote highly detailed essays on literature and philosophy. I wrote poems and dreamed of making my mark on the world as a writer. My English literature teacher Sister Lisa Mary (her initials expanded to "SLIM" behind her back) had us try out Faulkner's free association technique. Part of what I wrote was, "I know the inside world quite well but not the outside…In a psychological study they said children are not as aware as adults, they live in a daze well I'm still a child then but in 'socially acceptable ways' in that I am a would-be writer. That's why I'm proud of my introspective impression." But as far as dealing with feelings, the unspoken mantra growing up was, "Don't feel! Don't feel! Or at the very least put your feelings on hold." And so, deprived of my emotional legacy, as a young child I coped by withdrawing—not the healthiest strategy I well realize, but one of the few available to me at the time. I spent a lot of time alone and was shy around most people. On the plus side, I think my withdrawing deeply into myself made for the rich internal world that subsequently gave me the makeup for being a chaplain, writer, and teacher.

Left primarily to my own devices I kept myself going during my college years by setting high academic goals plus the extensive travelling I had done including Puerto de la Libertad in El Salvador and Kurashiki, Japan, where I had taught English as a Second Language. Looking back, I had put my writing and love of words into an academic straitjacket which I did not toss away until I resumed my creative writing four decades later in my mid-fifties.

Despite my achievements, including Phi Beta Kappa and graduating with highest honors from Oberlin College, the lack of the proper taking in and letting out of emotions had taken an exorbitant toll, which only became greater as time went on. For most people, feeling emotions is as automatic as breathing. For me, I have to often remind myself to be in touch with what I am feeling. It was only through the gentle ongoing work of several compassionate therapists and friends that by my fifties I was at last able to claim the nonintellectual part of my inheritance that every child has a right to.

A couple of weeks later, Darleen drops in for our second visit. It takes me a little longer than last time to rise from my cushioned chair, go step by step to the door, and tug it open. I am stubborn about programming it to open on its own; I do not want technology to coddle me to death like in Stanislaw Lem's cautionary tales about the search for happiness in his science fiction work *The Cyberiad*. I offer her some tea and dried fruit and then sit back down to wait and see what she will say. A little contest of silence ensues between us until she asks, "What are you thinking about now?" I reply with a chuckle that I am waiting for her to speak first since that was what I was used to doing when I was a chaplain to ensure that clients would talk about what they needed to talk about. Darleen chuckles in return and then skillfully takes that to a meaningful level: "What do *you* need to talk about?"

I do not especially feel like digging too much psychologically, or releasing the tears demanding their exit upon hearing her words, but her simply asking me what I need is a hook. It is not often that someone wants to stay the course with me past the small talk, so despite some fatigue I soldier on. "As a child, I had to fall back on my own world. Like I said, my mother was busy with her coterie, and my father had his own preoccupations, so they could not emotionally be around for me very often. There hardly ever were any wholesome people around. I remember whenever I saw an unexpected car pull into our driveway, my spirits rose as I wondered who could be visiting us, but every time the car pulled back out because the driver was only there to turn around and go in the opposite direction,which left me marooned once again. I was left to my own devices and did not fit in to the social world of other children. And so I was betwixt and between, neither fully here nor there, neither fully within the family circle at home nor in the wider world outside the home."

Darleen interrupts. "You know, there is a really, really sad paragraph in your "Upward Spiral" story—I went back after our last visit and looked it up—about your feeling shut out. You know which one I mean?"

"I sure do; that was a true part about when my Mom locked me outside for a little while so she could yak on the phone." I get a copy of the story on my nearby screen, direct it to the right paragraphs, and I show it to Darleen. She reads it out loud: "'When I was about eight, Mom had me go in the back porch and she locked not one but both parts of the Dutch door that stood between it and the dining room. I banged and banged on the window and hollered to be let in. How I loathed the idea that she willfully kept talking and kept ignoring me as if I were not standing out there. Nothing, not my voice nor even my outraged tears, reached her as her laughter applauded the merry comments of her friend.'"

I sigh; I sure do sound forlorn there. Darleen looks at me to see how this registers on me. I sigh again and say, "As nasty as my mother sounds there, in the long run it was a good thing that she shut me out sometimes. Being in the family circle was not a good place for me to be. I began to sense later on that I not only did not want to be included, but that I wanted to steer way clear of it. I guess I got used to looking at just about everything at a distance: my family, children at school, other adults. So later in life, I think that's why I liked taking the stance of an observer. I used to love studying anthropology; I could relate to how the researcher talked about their 'subjects.' Chaplaincy, and writing too, is about closely observing the world, which takes some distancing."

Darleen nods her understanding and finishes off her by now tepid tea. She is a good sport to do that; I like mine steaming hot. She responds, "I think the distancing you're talking about has kept you good and far from the edge of the pit. That scary dangerous pit."

I am uneasy; she is bringing me near that pit again which I have worked all my life to edge away from and not topple back into. It's one thing to live along the edge, quite another to lose balance and go over it, or even linger there too long. I say, "This makes me think about the Joseph story, where his brothers throw him into a pit. There's no water in it, and maybe predators could go there and have themselves a feast."

"Speaking of food," she replies, "you know what happens next in the story. The very next thing is that the Bible says his brothers went and had a meal! Who could eat after doing what they did to their own brother, which was more or less a death sentence?"

"Worse than that," I say, "I remember some commentator said the brothers quickly walked far from the pit and got busy with other things so they wouldn't hear Joseph's cries of distress." I feel myself simmering, my own distress surging through my flushed skin. My anger mounts as I recalled my inability for my anguish to get through to my parents, to either one. "Not only was I left in the pit, not only did my parents walk away, they came back over to make sure I stayed down there! They did not want me to escape. They could not escape their own pit which they were in, and they wanted me to stay next door in my own. But I did escape anyway. Maybe a vestige of me remains in it, but damn it, I clambered out and helped many people out of their own pits. Yes, that is what I did! And that is what my story you just read from is about." All of a sudden, spent, I feel a fierce urge to sleep, and I have to tell Darleen I am too tired to talk anymore. "You're welcome to stay, but I won't be very interesting to you asleep." I'm only half joking.

As I drift off, not too concerned whether Darleen is still there or not, I think about how I have explained the story title "Upward Spiral." It's about what I just said to Darleen. It suggests a positive although ambivalent journey to a better emotional and spiritual place. The many circuitous turns of the narrator in her journey, which of course was psychologically my own, hampered my progress. My own resistance and that of others added to the steepness of the climb. There were my downward moments, but more or less I kept to an upward pattern. I think too about Joseph in the pit, and how he ultimately made it out of there emotionally as well as physically. Not only that, he transcended his shortcomings to forgive his family and rescue them and countless others from famine.

A couple of weeks after the chaplain's previous visit, I hear the welcome knock on the door. I do not mind that my husband saves me the trouble of having to make the long trek all the way there to open it. As she comes in, she greets him with a hug before he goes off to another room. He senses that I need some private time to talk with her as does he, as he had done last time after I fell asleep. This visit she recognizes that the length of time I can talk at each visit is shorter, understanding that I must spend my verbal coins economically. So Darleen gets down to important matters. "What's most on your mind today?" she asks. I do not take the easy way out by wasting the offering of rich interaction by mentioning something mundane like what I would be eating for dinner. I figure I might as well give her a run for her money and go for the really deep stuff: "I think the path of my life has been one long contest between breaking free of anxiety and embracing the moment. Anxiety has robbed me of peace and joy. I often missed out on the riches of the moment." My tears demand their freedom and finally win it right while I am saying this to her.

After the reluctant teardrops all land peacefully on my hand-embroidered shirt, she quotes the poet Debbie Perlman, "'Your tears are jewels.'"

As more jewels join their fellows upon my shirt, I feel my head clear. I suddenly want to tell her my latest conclusions about God: "You know what I think God is all about? God is not a commander, or a being who rescues people or doesn't rescue people. God does not grant wishes or punish or watch indifferently from up high. God is here wherever living things forge a connection between each other that brings out their best or lets them be authentic. I think God is about what makes living things want to continue living and drives nonliving things to become living ones. Like when I connected in an authentic way with my patients, and of course with my husband Steve, and when people like you are connecting with me, God is here. Even when we make healing connections within ourselves that help us know ourselves more and care more about ourselves and others, that's when God is present. Or maybe I should say I am more aware of God's presence at such moments. I believe God is always present, but usually unnoticed and somehow subconsciously registered in the brain. You know, this is like the instruments in an orchestra that play the background parts that enrich the sounds of the ones playing the melody, and act as a backdrop for the soloists."

"You say you feel a Presence right now, with us?" she asks.

"Yes," I respond, "because I do feel myself clutching at these remaining moments of life. Even now, I feel as if you, this room, this house, all the loved ones in it, all my previous thoughts and memories of all connection are receding. They are getting smaller as if I were in a train, seated facing the caboose, feeling pulled backwards and ever further away from all of this as the train speeds forward."

Darleen and I sit placidly in the quiet for a very long time. Steve comes back in to join the welcoming silence. Steve and I have always liked interludes of quiet. I take in the small noises in the background. The wind is rattling the impatient leaves. A lawn mower's bass voice crescendos and decrescendos as it mows nearer, then further, then nearer again, off and on drowning out the bird calls—these sounds and movements are richer than any symphony and as dramatic as any action film. I see sparrows in the wake of the mower's progress go in a jagged line of jumps contrasted with the obedient steady itinerary of passersby on the boardwalk. I feel the rise and fall of my chest and abdomen as I breathe, all of this sensation as infinitely captivating as the exotica of my extensive travels. Quiet places have been my refuge and my meeting place for fanning my internal flame of passion. The silence here is sacred, beheld reverently by us as I prepare to dwell in the burgeoning stillness to come.

Acknowledgments

In order of their influence upon the creation of and reshaping of this book, I would like to express my appreciation to the following: To my husband Steven, who throughout my seven years as a hospice chaplain kept asking me when I would get around to writing down my encounters with "all those interesting people from all walks of life;" to the Reverend Deborah K. Davis, formerly my Princeton Hospice supervisor, whose psychological wisdom helped me access the deeper levels of my career choice; to Ruth of Ruth Mills Literary Services, who challenged me to lengthen and strengthen the manuscript before I submitted it to publishers; to my friend Lilly Napolitano, who heard me read every single word aloud and pounced on any confusing phrases; to the Angry Bean Coffeehouse Writers' Group of North Arlington, New Jersey, who helped me come up with the title; to Kelsey Rice, who translated the essence and perspective of this book into the welcoming visual language of the cover design; and to Duke and Kimberly Pennell of Pen-L Publishing, who humored me by answering a whole book's worth of questions from the time of submission to the heady days of "going live" with this memoir.

KAREN B. KAPLAN, April 2014

In Memoriam: Jack Rodney
October 15, 1956—April 4, 2014

My very close friend for decades, Jack found humor in the unlikeliest of subjects, including his own demise. Once I became ordained, he loved to say, "Now you can do my funeral."

I did not end up doing that but I was able to add this memorial page in the nick of time. Jack died about one week prior to the publication of *Encountering the Edge*. May this page comfort friends and family.

About the Author

Karen B. Kaplan served as a hospice chaplain for seven years, working at United Hospice of Rockland in New York and Princeton Hospice in New Jersey. Since then, her focus has shifted exclusively to writing. She has a published novella plus numerous short stories and articles and teaches essay writing to ESL students at Hudson County Community College in Union City, NJ. She also heads The Angry Coffee Bean Café Writers' Group. Her next work will be a collection of "Compassionate Science Fiction" short stories (this means no swords and no murderous robots).

OFFBEATCOMPASSION.COM